ILLUSTRATORS 16

The Sixteenth Annual National Exhibition
of Illustration held in the
Galleries of the Society of Illustrators
128 East 63rd Street, New York
February 14 through April 19, 1974

ILLUSTRATORS 16

The Sixteenth
Annual of American Illustration
Published for the Society of Illustrators
Designed & Edited by Walter Brooks
Hastings House, Publishers, Inc.,
New York 10016

Illustrators 16

Chairman	Robert Cuevas
Assistant Chairman	Roland Descombes
Designer of Call for Entries & Announcement	Robert Cuevas
Illustrator of Call for Entries & Announcement	Mark English
Hanging Chairman	Charles Long
Awards Luncheon Chairman	Roland Descombes
Awards Luncheon Speakers	Richard Hess Paul Dobler
Treasurer	Charles McVicker
Editor/Designer of Annual Book	Walter Brooks
Staff	Andrea Herrick Gabe Herrick Cathy Groff Terry Brown Norma Pimsler Arpi Ermoyan

Contents

ISBN: 8038-3397-0

Library of Congress Catalog Card Number: 59-10849

Printed in the United States of America

Distributors:
CANADA Saunders of Toronto Ltd., Don Mills, Ontario
GREAT BRITAIN Transatlantic Book Service, Ltd., 7 Maiden Lane, London WC2E 7NA
AUSTRIA, GERMANY AND SWITZERLAND Arthur Niggli, Ltd., Bohl, 9052 Niederteufen AR, Switzerland
FRANCE Editions Paralleles, 172 rue Pelleport, Paris XXe
All other countries Fleetbooks c/o Feffer and Simons, Inc., 100 Park Avenue, New York, NY 10017

Bill Shields

The President's Message

Those with a certain philosophic viewpoint equate a picture with a thousand words…thus, we present you with this concise five-hundred-thousand word volume. If you are perceptive enough to decipher its contents you will uncover your own plot—there are many—subtly intertwined. Use it for stimulating skimming or profound perusal as poetry, a catalogue or a history. Visual statements do not readily succumb to verbal categorizing. It is a permanent record of a fine exhibit that graced the walls of the Society's galleries as the result of the efforts of thousands of entrants, forty jurors, the Annual Show Committee, the designer and editor and the S.I. staff. Please treat it gently, much love has gone into its creation.

Shannon Stirnweis

The Chairman's Statement

I would like to thank the Society of Illustrators for giving me the distinction of being the 16th Annual Show Chairman. It gave me the opportunity to work side by side with some of the finest people I've known.

It took many wonderful and talented artists and designers, working many hours to assemble it, and without their help, this exciting challenge could not have been achieved.

Barnett Plotkin

Robert Cuevas

The Designer/Editor's Comment

The logistics of turning the annual show into the annual book don't change much as the years go on. The assignment is pretty well stabilized, after 15 years, as a perpetual fantastic challenge which reduces grown men and, soon we hope, women into whimpering creatures hovering over wall-to-wall 8 x 10's. Geissmann, Munce, and all my other predecessors have spelled it out. The show is the message and, if the designer does his job well, the book is a valid, conscientious, permanent echo. Thanks to Jim Moore of Hastings House, Jerry McConnell, Walt Reed, and all of the other official artists from the Society who contributed so generously of their time. I might add that the editor this year was extremely cooperative.

Walter Brooks

Harry Bennett

Harry Carter

CARL BOBERTZ 1899-1974

When Carl Bobertz was president of the Society of Illustrators in 1964 and 1965 he once said, "If you are going to make a speech you had better have something you really want to say, or you had better keep quiet and not bore people. And that goes for painting pictures too." This comes as close as anything he ever said in public to suggest his personal philosophy of art and life.

Speaking now of this gentle man we must defer to his simply stated cautionary truth and strive for the words that will best describe the unaffected quality of his particular way of living well. To impose a public image on a life that was essentially private will not at all serve the purpose. Carl lived in a world of kindliness and grace. His was not a complex nature; he was, if anything, a fundamentalist. There was a basis, an essential belief, in everything he did and said. His integrity was unbreachable, and compromise in questions of honesty was simply not possible for him.

The historical facts of his life do not astound us. Born in Detroit, of strong, transplanted Hanoverian stock, he set out from his earliest years to become an artist. The climate was encouraging; his mother *hoped* he would favor music as a career but was not unhappy when his interests developed into more visual ways of expression. Even so, surviving family memorabilia attest to recitals and public concert programs that list Carl Bobertz as violinist. Indeed, his violin and record turntable, never more than three feet from his drawingboard, indicate how closely throughout the years he equated music with his art.

Records indicate that Wayne University had him for a while, but that was abruptly terminated with the call to soldiering. The year was 1918. With the Armistice, he returned to his studies and his formal art education began, and continued, ending only with his death in the early Spring of 1974.

Coming to New York in 1941 from a well-established advertising art career in Detroit he found immediate acceptance as a fiction illustrator for magazines such as *Collier's, American Magazine, McCall's* and others. At the same time, his unpretentious and direct style was sought after by advertising and textbook art directors. Work in this latter field occupied much of his time to the last.

A devotion to the Society of Illustrators, from his election to membership in 1943 and throughout the years since, was implicit in his thirty years of cheerful and willing service to that organization. There was hardly a committee on which he did not serve. He gave his best to all, but his particular pleasure was in the chairmanship of the Joint Ethics Committee. A believer in orderly, democratic procedure, he worked for years rewriting and checking the Constitution and By-laws of the Society, and has been affectionately called Godfather to that impressive document.

The Warwick Training School for Boys saw him frequently as a volunteer, guiding the young to the intricate ways of the artist in the Art Workshop. Veteran Hospital Portraits Project was another of his favored public services. In 1946 alone, he completed 34 portraits of hospitalized veterans which were then sent as gifts to the parents of the sitters.

Two particular achievements in which he took great pride must now be mentioned. The 1960 painting *Air Rescue Mission in Alaska* done for the Air Force Historical Art Archives is an excellent example of his best style. He, himself, considered it one of his finest works. In the same year, he was commissioned to design the *Employ the Handicapped* Commemorative Stamp for the United States Post Office Department. This humanitarian theme that appears with regularity throughout the career of Carl Bobertz is also to be noted, for it was not accidental. He felt strongly a responsibility toward others less advantaged, and his reward was the pleasure he received being allowed the use of his talent in this service.

Harry Carter

THE HAMILTON KING AWARD

The Hamilton King Award is given each year to a member of the Society of Illustrators who, in the opinion of a selected jury, has achieved the highest degree of excellence for a specific piece of art created during that year.

The Hamilton King Award for 1974 was bestowed upon FRED OTNES for his 3' x 6' assemblage titled "Discovering American History" which was commissioned by Holt, Rinehart & Winston.

Mr. Otnes attended the Chicago Art Institute and the American Academy. He has been noted for his use of the collage and assemblage technique. A member of the Society since 1970, he presently lives in West Redding, Connecticut.

Previous winners are:

1965	Paul Calle
1966	Bernie Fuchs
1967	Mark English
1968	Robert Peak
1969	Alan Cober
1970	Ray Ameijide
1971	Miriam Schottland
1972	Charles Santore
1973	Dave Blossom

The Hall of Fame Awards

Since 1958 the past presidents of the Society, along with the Hall of Fame committee chairman, have elected those to receive our industry's highest honor, the Society of Illustrators Hall of Fame Award. This year it was felt that the awards should be expanded to include both living and deceased artists and that more than one artist could be selected.

The awards for "distinguished achievement in the art of illustration" for 1974 were presented to TOM LOVELL and posthumously to CHARLES DANA GIBSON and NEWELL CONVERS WYETH.

A brief biography written especially for the presentation ceremonies follows:

TOM LOVELL. When he works, Tom Lovell wears an ancient denim apron which over the years has caught a rain of splashes, drips, wipes, swipes and smears of paint. It has become so rigid he could get out of it by merely bending his knees and backing off. I relate this not to reveal the laundry secrets of the Lovell household, but as a bridge to illuminate an incident I once witnessed there. I arrived on a Sunday morning a bit earlier than I was expected. Tom's wife called into the bedroom to announce me. He emerged in a few minutes *already wearing his apron.* I have to conclude that either he wears break-away pajamas or he keeps a second easel at the foot of his bed. As you can see, this man is not your every-day dilettante. Thomas Lovell comes to *paint!* He started doing just that forty years ago after a short stint at sea and four years of art training at Syracuse University. For the last many of these years, his peers and the public have highly approved of his output. That has to be a special satisfaction to have the touch to reach people who don't know why they're being reached—and to stir professionals who know very well. Tom's native ability has been trained and honed throughout his life. During the last part of his study at Syracuse he contributed frequently to the pulps. And he contributed more to *them* than they did to him since they paid $7.00 per *full page!* Six years later he was doing the illustrations in the slick books for the stories of Ferber, Gallico, Bromfield and Sinclair Lewis. Then came the War, his enlistment and a memorable series of historic paintings for the Marine Corps.

And since then, difficult and demanding pictures for National Geographic and others. These pictures need to be historically accurate. And indeed, they wind up being. He doesn't stop until facts are pinned down, authenticated, verified and *notarized.* When he can't find a prop, he makes it—according to known specifications. He's the Beaver's beaver. It's appropriate that Tom's Hall of Fame Award occurs on the same night that the newly instituted older Greats Awards are beginning. It's appropriate because he represents a link with the realistic story-telling illustrators of the past. Key men in his development have been Remington, Russell, Pyle, Dunn…and above all Von.

Tom Lovell is one of the last of the long line of men who have painted the heroic, adventurous, swashbuckling world of history and rousing fiction. He has said that he loved to read and dream of those things when he was a boy. Happily he got to be one of those lucky men who has lived his fantasy his whole life through. And he's got a dirty apron to prove it!   *Howard Munce*

CHARLES DANA GIBSON, N.A. (1867-1944) The "American Girl" has been extolled in countless ways since, but never better than in the pen-and-ink drawings by Gibson in the Victorian Era. The Gibson Girl was not one but many types of girls—each imbued with an ideal refinement that most women could secretly identify with and all men admire. Gibson Girls blossomed everywhere—in popular songs, on banners, pillow cases, even silver spoons, and Gibson's drawings were carefully studied and copied for the latest hair styling and costume. Although those transient styles have long ago disappeared, Gibson's work has a validity that keeps his pictures from being dated. He recorded his times objectively enough for us to see the frailties of the social values, yet with a warmth and sympathy that helps us to understand and respect them. Gibson's work first appeared in the old *LIFE* Magazine and in 1904, a contract with *COLLIER'S WEEKLY* made him the highest paid illustrator in America. Collections of his drawings appeared periodically in a series of books that ran into many editions. As president of the Society of Illustrators during World War I he served as head of the Division of Pictorial Publicity under the Federal Committee of Public Information. Under its direction, some illustrators were sent overseas as war correspondents, others helped in the preparation of posters, billboards, illustrations and other forms of publicity on behalf of the war effort.

NEWELL CONVERS WYETH, N.A. (1885-1945) Although he was better known as N. C. Wyeth, as he signed his pictures with bold strokes, Wyeth's powerful, dramatic illustrations need not have been signed at all to be recognized as unmistakably his. Wyeth had a unique, original talent, encouraged and nurtured by his master, Howard Pyle. As part of his schooling, he went West in 1904 to work as a cowhand and to draw and paint among the Indians. He returned East with a reservoir of experience that enabled him to launch his illustration career with a series of Indian paintings for OUTING Magazine that were sensationally successful. From that time on, for nearly forty years, Wyeth was one of America's busiest and best known illustrators. His work appeared in all of the major magazines and for numerous book publishers. Over a period of years, he illustrated more than twenty-five books in the Charles Scribner's Sons' classics series for titles such as *Treasure Island, The Black Arrow,* and *Mysterious Island.* He also painted for exhibition and encouraged his children to follow artistic careers. He will be equally well remembered as the founder of the Wyeth artistic family, which includes his daughters, Ann, a composer, Henriette and Caroline, his son, Andrew, and grandson, James, all of whom have pursued painting careers.   *Walt Reed*

Previous Hall of Fame recipients are:

AMERICAN ILLUSTRATION–HOW IT WAS By Walt Reed

Illustration has always had the habit of looking forward, seldom back. A typical young illustrator or student is properly concerned with what is going on today—or will happen tomorrow. If he thinks about the past at all, it is apt to be in terms of the passé— something to be rejected. Yet, his work could only be enriched by discovering some of the marvelous pictures that have been produced by his dedicated predecessors.

Actually, American Illustration has a short history. If counted from the introduction of photo-engraving for reproduction, it is less than a century old. Earlier illustrators, if no less talented, were rendered almost anonymously alike by wood engravers who transposed their original drawings or paintings into scribed woodblock facsimiles for printing. Even Winslow Homer's double-page spreads in *Harper's Weekly* show little of his technical skill. In many cases the illustrators drew or painted directly on the wood blocks so that the originals were literally cut to pieces in the engraving process.

Those whose careers overlapped the transition from wood engraving to photo engraving, however, revealed themselves to be highly individualized illustrators and consummate craftsmen.

A. B. Frost, Charles S. Rinehart, Charles Dana Gibson, Edwin Austin Abbey and Howard Pyle all bridged the two periods and were the progenitors of the "Golden Age of Illustration." The profession grew and flourished spectacularly with the parallel growth of the national magazines and national advertisers who subsidized them. Many of America's finest artists were attracted to this huge new market for pictures.

Of this early group, Howard Pyle was in a class by himself and no one has ever surpassed him. A master storyteller in words as well as in pictures, he wrote and illustrated tales of pirates, medieval knighthood and other historical subjects, and illustrated works by the prominent authors of his day. Some of his most important pictures were published in books, such as Woodrow Wilson's fine volume, *History of the American People*. He also had a profound impact on illustration through his many students.

One of his most original pupils was N. C. (Newell Convers) Wyeth. Wyeth's forte was drama and he distilled his ideas through an intense personality. The frontier life of the homesteader, the sheep herder, the prospector and the cowboy appealed to him, and he recorded the American Indian with unusual dignity and

H. Pyle

insight in an early series of paintings. Like Pyle, he was at his best as a storyteller, and his ability to dramatize key episodes in classic adventure stories was highly appreciated by thousands of children and their parents who read to them.

A prominent contemporary of Wyeth's—but diametrically opposed in outlook—was Charles Dana Gibson. Gibson, who was urbane, worldly and witty, recorded the fashionable world of the post-Victorian era. His "Gibson Girl" epitomized the ideal American girl and millions of women tried to emulate her appearance. And, Gibson's clean-shaven men doomed the moustache and beard. His humorous, satiric pictures, collected in several volumes, humanize the history of his time as no words can.

The list of all the rest, from the beginning of the century to the present, is too long to give due respect here, but in this period of women's emancipation, some of the outstanding female illustrators must be mentioned. In the Victorian Era, most art schools barred women from life classes. Their talents were steered to the home arts and decoration, and it took a determined woman to pursue a professional illustration career.

One of the earliest was Mary Hallock Foote, who made some excellent illustrations of the Old West, particularly of early California, for *Century* and other magazines in the 1880s and '90s. May Wilson Preston studied under Whistler in Paris and had a long illustration career which continued until the 1930s. Alice Barber Stephens began as a wood engraver for *Scribner's* and graduated to a career as portrait painter and illustrator.

Howard Pyle encouraged his female students and an unusually large number of them had long, successful illustration careers. Among them were: Elizabeth Shippen Green, Anna Whelan Betts, Charlotte Harding, Sarah S. Stillwell (Weber) and Jessie Willcox Smith.

Most women gravitated to subjects involving women, babies and children. Maud Tousey Fangel specialized in babies and her pastel drawings made from life are beautifully spontaneous. Rose O'Neill, as an illustrator of children, developed a series of elf-like baby characters who inspired children to exemplary conduct. These "Kewpies" became a national institution with a special monthly page allotted to them in the *Ladies Home Journal* and *Good Housekeeping* Magazine for many years, and Kewpie dolls were sold in the millions. Clara Elsene Peck regularly illustrated stories and articles on family life, child-rearing and psychology. Maginel Wright Barney, sister of Frank Lloyd Wright,

N. C. Wyeth

C. D. Gibson

M. H. Foote

was also a prolific illustrator of children's subjects. Irma Deremeaux covered a whole range of subject matter: her lively illustrations having the immediacy of reportorial drawings.

Neysa McMein had a special position in the New York social scene where her studio was a gathering place for actors, dancers, poets, novelists and other artists. Alexander Wollcott, Bea Lillie, Dorothy Parker and Irving Berlin were among the many regular visitors. In spite of the distractions she illustrated for most major magazines, including monthly covers for *McCall's* for many years and made pastel portraits of prominent women of various professions.

Most illustrators, male or female, were too busy to realize it at the time but their interpretations of the contemporary scene for fiction or editorial articles were creating an historic record. For the most part, this record is now confined to back issues of the magazines; the originals, once reproduced, were considered to be of little value to either the publication or the artist and the great body of them have disappeared. *The Saturday Evening Post* regularly gave originals to interested advertisers upon request and donated many canvases to a Philadelphia art school for students to paint over. One prominent illustrator turned over his canvases for his sons to use for target practice. Neighbor

M. W. Preston

A. B. Stephens

E. S. Green

A. W. Betts

C. Harding

S. S. Stillwell (Weber)

J. W. Smith

children of another illustrator used his originals on illustration board as bases for softball games!

Gradually, however, art scholars and museums are beginning to recognize the validity of illustration as an art form. Recently the Brooklyn Museum held an important Illustration Retrospective Show; the Wilmington Museum, a major Howard Pyle Show; Yale University, an Edwin Austin Abbey exhibition; the New Britain Museum, an annual showing of additions to their Illustration Collection; and the Bruce Museum of Greenwich held an exhibition of A. B. Frost's paintings.

Commercial galleries have had sales and exhibitions of works by Norman Rockwell (which have gone on a world tour), James Montgomery Flagg, Russell Patterson and Charles Sarka. Harold Von Schmidt had a one-man show at the Cowboy Hall of Fame in Oklahoma City, and the Brandywine Museum at Chadd's Ford has exhibited the Pyle School as well as the Wyeths. Interest in Western illustration, which began early with Frederic Remington and Charles Russell, generated a rediscovery of Henry Farny, Charles Schreyvogel and other early illustrators of the West.

Several books have been published on illustrators' careers and others are in preparation. The handsomest and most prepossessing is Tom Buechner's *Norman Rockwell*, published by Abrams; there are other excellent volumes on the work of Maxfield Parrish, N. C. Wyeth, John Held, Jr., A. B. Frost, Harold Von Schmidt and Harvey Dunn.

How will posterity react to today's illustration? Now, perhaps more than at any previous time, the illustrator has an opportunity to react to his subjects, to record the social scene and to make a personal comment on it with a far greater degree of freedom than his predecessors. If at times in the past the gap between fine and commercial art had been an almost unbridgeable one, today it is little more than a footpath that can be crossed almost at will by the illustrator with something important to say. Not every assignment offers an equal artistic potential, of course, but creative ingenuity will find a way to go beyond the requirements of an incidental episode in a piece of fiction or product in an advertising campaign. That is the test that has been passed by the previous great illustrators who are honored in our profession.

M. T. Fangel

R. O'Neill

C. E. Peck

M. W. Barney

I. Deremeaux

N. McMein

ILLUSTRATORS 16

The Juries

ADVERTISING   Mike Ramus, Chairman

Gloria McKeown, Mark English, Francois Colos, Randall Enos. Dick Kohfield, Franklin McMahon, Fred Harsh, Gene Federico.

EDITORIAL   Warren Rogers, Chairman

Gerry Contreras, Harry Schaare, Lorraine Fox, Hal Kearney, Burt Silverman, Joseph Veno, Tony Chen, Tony Palladino.

INSTITUTIONAL   Bill Shields, Chairman

Janet McCaffery, Van Kaufman, Gene Szafran, Alvin Grossman, Roger Kastel, William A. Smith, Bob LoGrippo, Richard Gangel.

BOOK   Gerald McConnell, Chairman

Saul Tepper, Dean Ellis, S. Neil Fujita, Garie Blackwell, Ed Brodkin, Elmer Pizzi, Roy Carruthers, Bob Anastasio.

TV OR FILM   Bob Jones, Chairman

Tom Yohe, Willis Pyle, Carl Fischer, Phil Kimmelman.

1
Institutional
*Artist/***Alan E. Cober**
Art Director/Harry O. Diamond
Client/Exxon Corp.
Gold Medal

2
Editorial
*Artist/***Brad Holland**
Art Director/Arthur Paul
Publication/Playboy Magazine

3
Editorial
*Artist/***Ken Dallison**
Art Director/Robert Hallock
Publication/Lithopinion

4
Advertising
*Artist/***Nick Aristovulos**
Art Director/Nick Aristovulos
Gold Medal

5
Book
*Artist/***Raymond Ameijide**
Art Director/Tom Von Der Linn
Title/Amahl and The Night Visitors
Publisher/Reader's Digest

6
Book
*Artist/***Gervasio Gallardo**
Art Director/Bob Blanchard
Title/Imaginary Worlds
Publisher/Ballantine Books, Inc.

7
Institutional
*Artist/***Linda Gist**
Art Director/Elmer Pizzi
Agency/Ray & Rogers
Client/Weyerhaeuser (Paper Division)

8
Editorial
*Artist/***Fred Otnes**
Art Director/Robert Hallock
Publication/Lithopinion

9
Advertising
*Artist/***John Freas**
Art Director/Dan Thomas

10
Book
*Artist/***Stan Hunter**
Art Director/Char Lappan
Title/Class
Publisher/Little, Brown & Co.

11
Advertising
*Artist/***Jim Conahan**
Art Director/Ken Krom & Jim Freeman
Agency/Leo Burnett Co., Inc.
Client/Philip Morris, Inc.

12
Advertising
*Artist/***Jim Conahan**
Art Director/Ken Krom & Jim Freeman
Agency/Leo Burnett Co., Inc.
Client/Philip Morris, Inc.

13
Institutional
*Artist/***Franklin McMahon**
Art Director/Steven Arnold
Client/Continental Illinois Co.

CAVENAGH BRIDGE
MAJ'R GENERAL ORFEUR CAVENAGH
GOVERNOR, STRAITS SETTLEMENTS
from 1859 to 1867

M. Johnson
Singapore

14
Advertising
*Artist/***Margot Zemach**
Art Director/Christine Stawicki
Client/The Children's Book Council

15
Editorial
*Artist/***Mark English**
Art Director/Alvin Grossman & Modesto Torre
Publication/McCall's Magazine

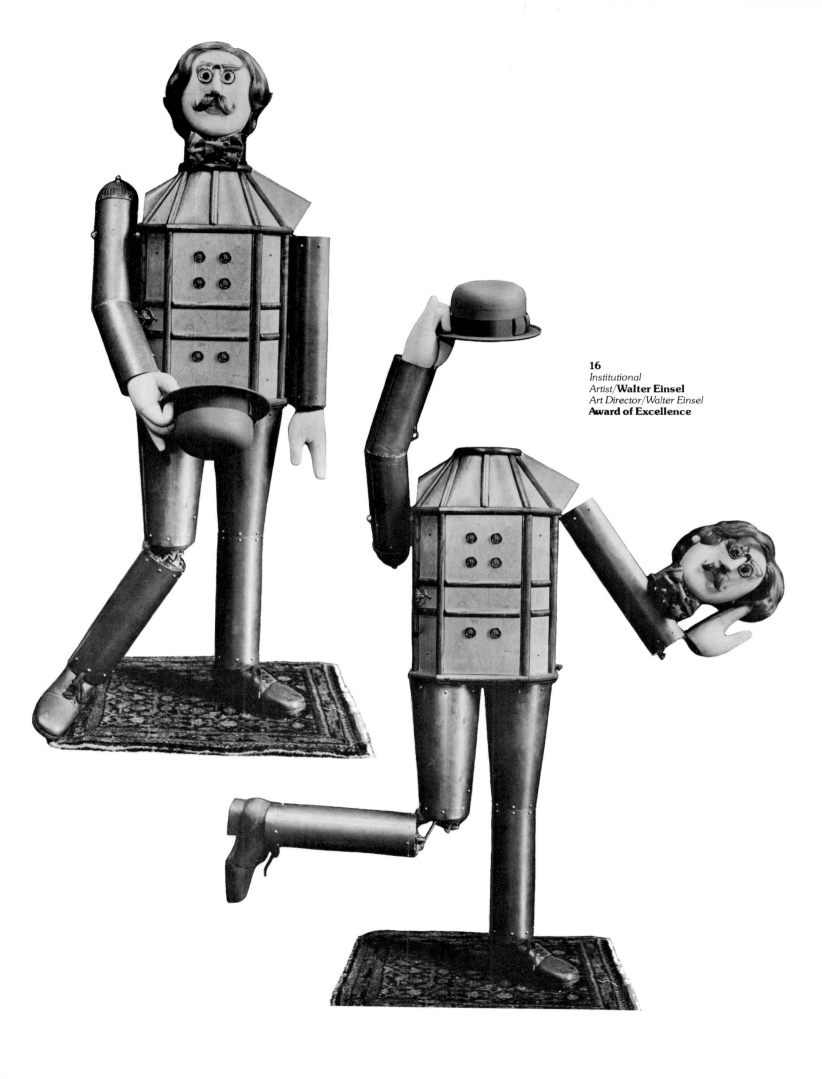

16
Institutional
*Artist/***Walter Einsel**
Art Director/Walter Einsel
Award of Excellence

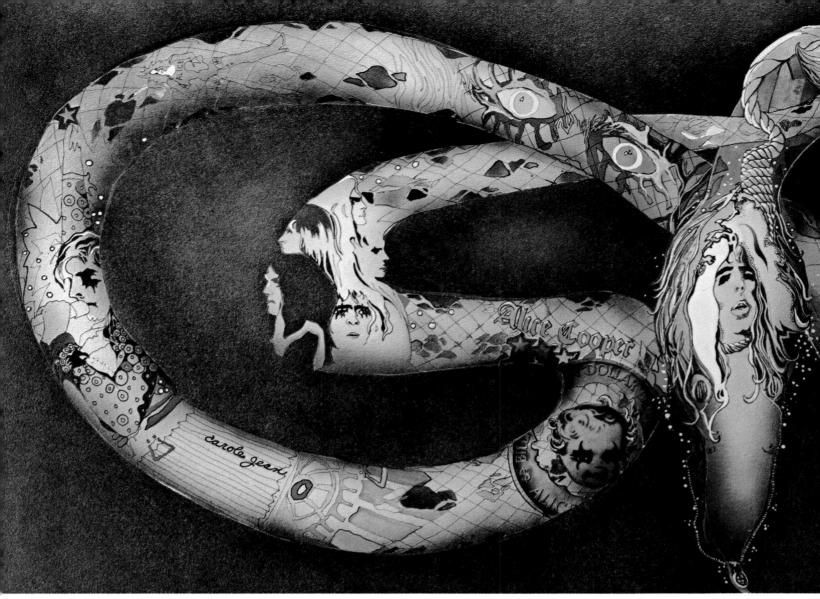

17
Advertising
*Artist/***Carole Jean (Feuerman)**
Art Director/Michael Neufeld
Client/Alosco & McLaughlin Enterprises, Inc.
Award of Excellence

18
Book
*Artist/***Fred Otnes**
Art Director/James Plumeri
Title/Horace
Publisher/New American Library

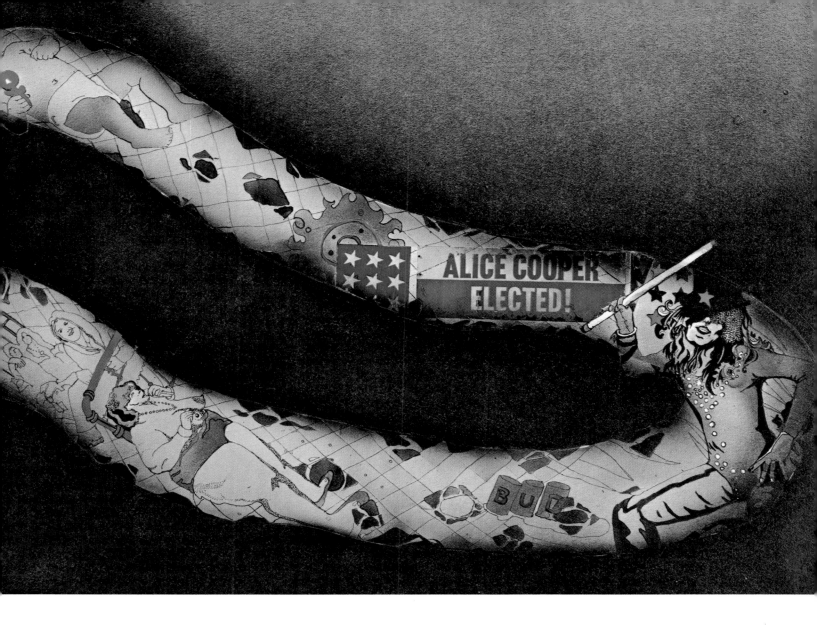

19
Editorial
*Artist/***Tom Hall**
Art Director/Ken Stuart & Don Hedin
Publication/Reader's Digest

20
Editorial
*Artist/***Lorraine Fox**
Art Director/Stan Mack
Publication/The New York Times

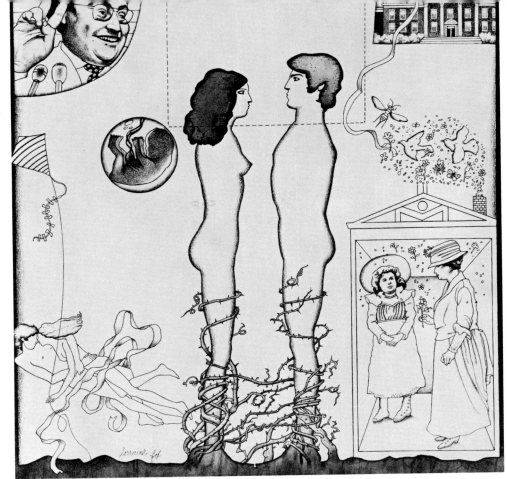

21
Editorial
*Artist/***William S. Shields**
Art Director/Bill Demlin
Publication/Market Publications

22
Book
*Artist/***Jean Leon Huens**
Art Director/K. Sneider & M. Miller
Title/Great People of the Bible
Publisher/Reader's Digest Association

23
Institutional
*Artist/***Rose Farber**
Art Director/Rose Farber
Agency/Hy Farber & Associates, Inc.
Client/Adstat & Adprint Co.

24
Advertising
*Artist/***James R. Crowell**
Art Director/Tom Tai
Agency/Young & Rubicam, Inc.
Client/Manufacturers Hanover Trust

25
Book
*Artist/***Joe Isom**
Art Director/William Gregory
Title/The Curse of the Kings
Publisher/Reader's Digest Association

26
Book
*Artist/***Sandy Kossin**
Art Director/William Gregory
Title/The Taking of Pelham One Two Three
Publisher/Reader's Digest Association

27
Institutional
Artist/**Charles McVicker**
Art Director/Charles McVicker

28
Book
Artist/**Tom Hall**
Art Director/Leonard Leone
Title/The Hessian
Publisher/Bantam Books, Inc.

29
Artist/**George S. Gaadt**
Art Director/Ron Chory
Agency/Fahlgren & Associates, Inc.
Client/Blue Cross

30
Book
*Artist/***Frank Frazetta**
Art Director/Bruce Hall
Title/The Silver Warriors
Publisher/Dell Publishing Co., Inc.

31
Book
*Artist/***Mark Alan Stamaty**
Art Director/Atha Tehon
Title/Who Needs Donuts?
Publisher/The Dial Press
Gold Medal

32
Advertising
*Artist/***David Palladini**
Art Director/Alan Davis
Client/London Records

33
Editorial
*Artist/***Donald M. Hedin**
Art Director/Ira Silberlicht
Publication/Emergency Medicine

34
Institutional
*Artist/***Robert Geissmann**
Art Director/Col. Russell Turner
Client/United States Air Force

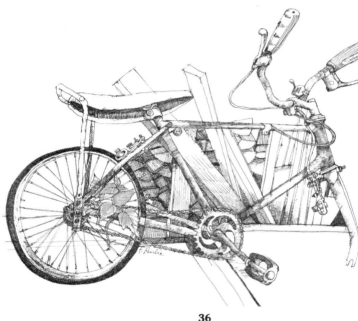

36
Institutional
*Artist/***Frank Renlie**
Art Director/Frank Renlie

35
Book
*Artist/***Dick Kramer**
Art Director/Dick Kramer

38
Film
*Artist/***Randall Enos**
Art Director/Gene Kolomatsky
Client/NBC

37
Book
*Artist/***Lew Friedland**
Art Director/Lew Friedland

39
Editorial
*Artist/***Wilson McLean**
Art Director/Richard M. Gangel
Publication/Sports Illustrated

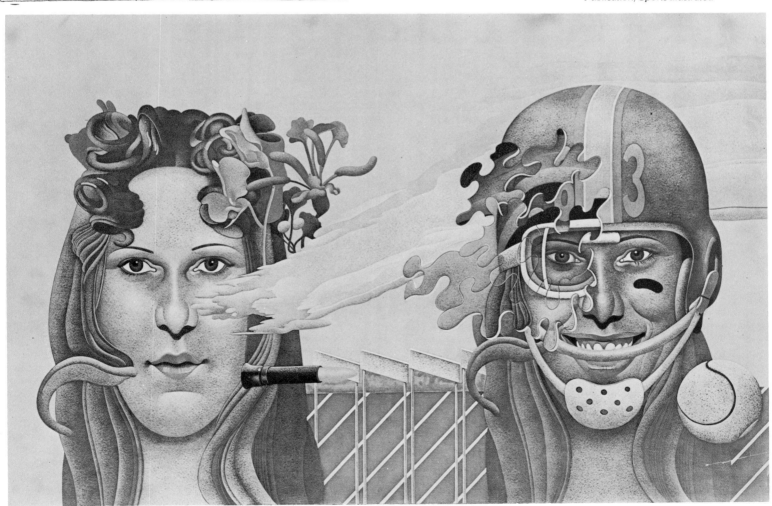

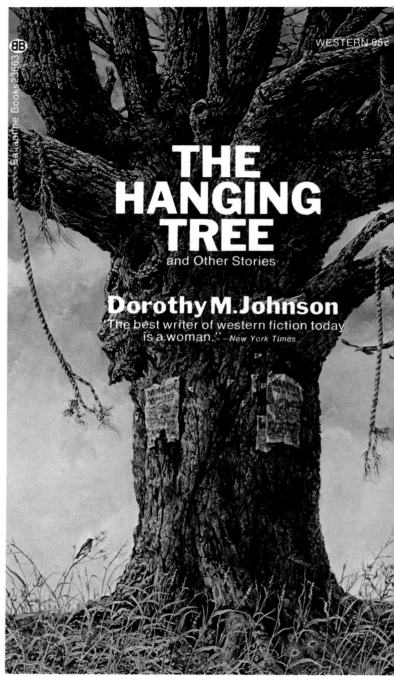

WESTERN 95¢

Ballantine Books 23563

THE HANGING TREE
and Other Stories

Dorothy M. Johnson
"The best writer of western fiction today
is a woman." —*New York Times*

40
Book
*Artist/***Gervasio Gallardo**
Art Director/Barbara Bertoli
Title/Nabokov's Dozen
Publisher/Avon Books

41
Book
*Artist/***Norman Adams**
Art Director/Bob Blanchard
Title/The Hanging Tree
Publisher/Ballantine Books, Inc.

42
Editorial
*Artist/***Gerald McConnell**
Art Director/Glenn Kipp
Publication/New Jersey Bell Magazine

43
Book
*Artist/***Jeffrey W. Cornell**
Art Director/Jeffrey W. Cornell

44
Institutional
*Artist/***Howard Rogers**
Art Director/Pete Ellebrect
Agency/Gardner Advertising Co.
Client/St. Louis Cardinals

45
Book
*Artist/***Ted Lewin**
Art Director/Cynthia Basil
Title/Lion on the Run
Publisher/Morrow Junior Books

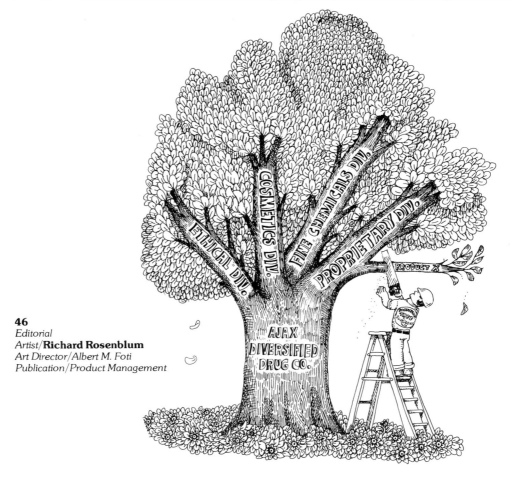

46
Editorial
Artist/**Richard Rosenblum**
Art Director/Albert M. Foti
Publication/Product Management

47
Advertising
Artist/**Charles Santore**
Art Director/Bob Ciano
Client/CTI Records

48
Book
*Artist/***Jim Jonson**
Art Director/Jim Jonson
Title/Tennis
Publisher/Prentice-Hall, Inc.

49
Book
*Artist/***Harry J. Schaare**
Art Director/Harry J. Schaare

50
Editorial
*Artist/***Daniel Schwartz**
Art Director/John C. Bradford
Publication/Family Circle

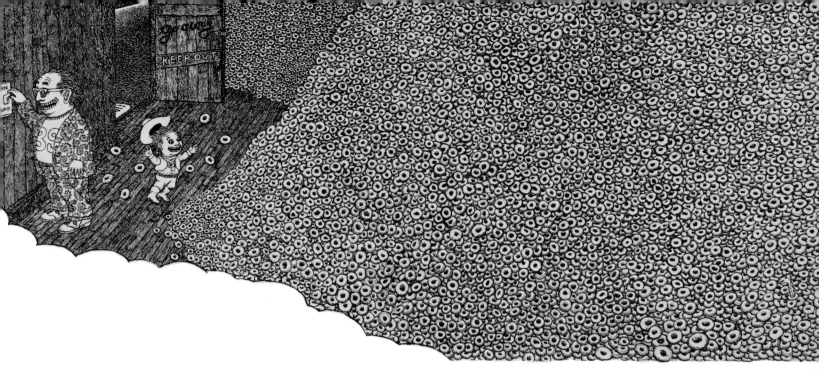

51
Book
*Artist/***Mark Alan Stamaty**
Art Director/Atha Tehon
Title/Who Needs Donuts?
Publisher/The Dial Press

52
Book
*Artist/***George Ziel**
Art Director/George Ziel

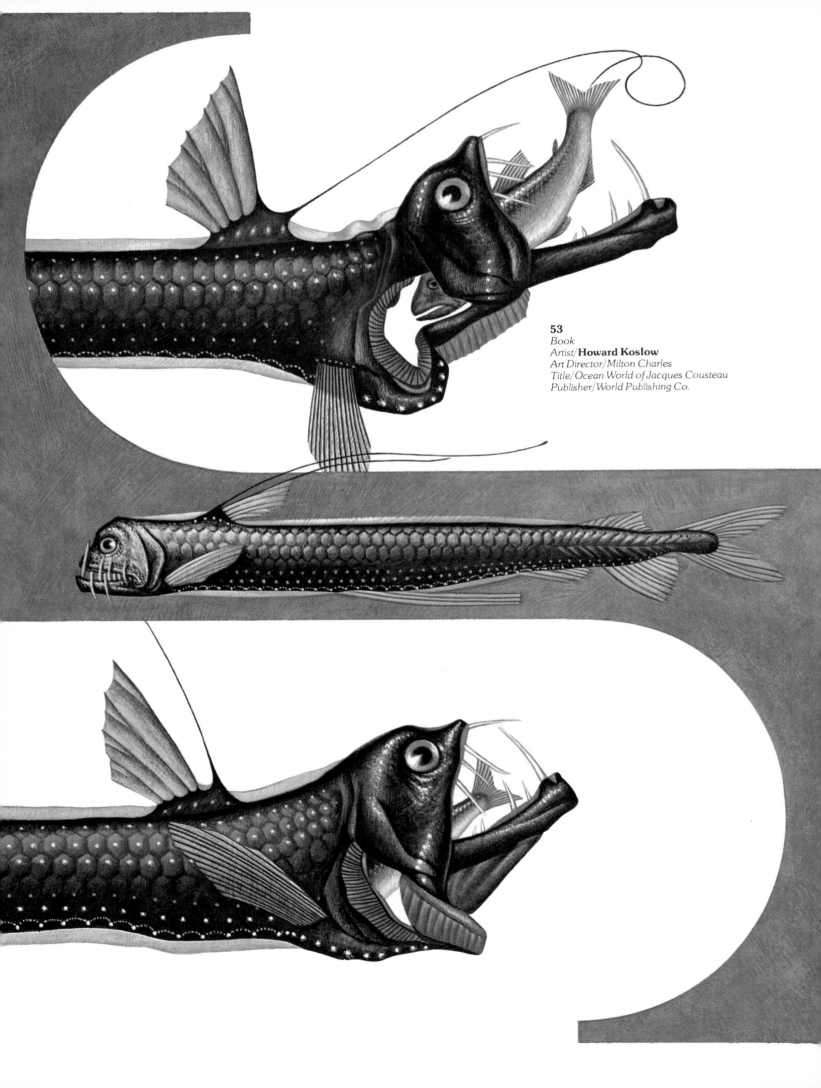

53
Book
Artist/ **Howard Koslow**
Art Director/Milton Charles
Title/Ocean World of Jacques Cousteau
Publisher/World Publishing Co.

54
Institutional
*Artist/***Ivan Chermayeff**
Art Director/Ivan Chermayeff
& Eugenia Lorenzo
Agency/Chermayeff & Geismar Associates
Client/National Endowment for the Arts

55
Advertising
*Artist/***Bob Alcorn**
Art Director/Bob Alcorn

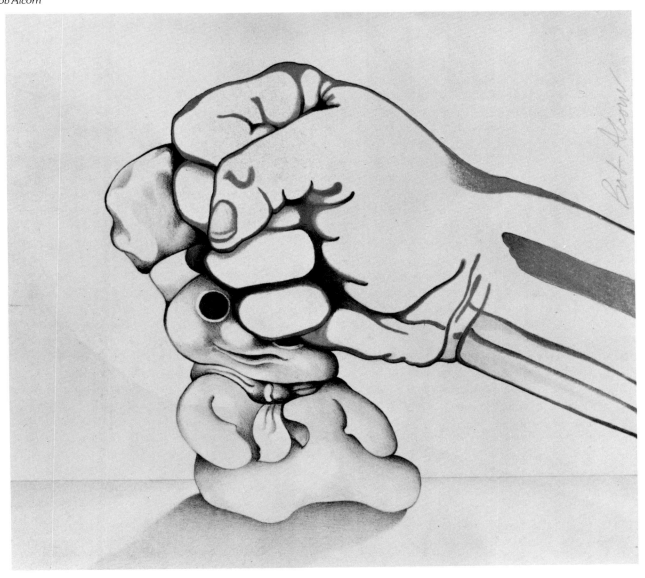

56
Book
*Artist/***Bart Forbes**
*Art Director/*Barbara Bertoli
Title/Paths of Glory
Publisher/Avon Books

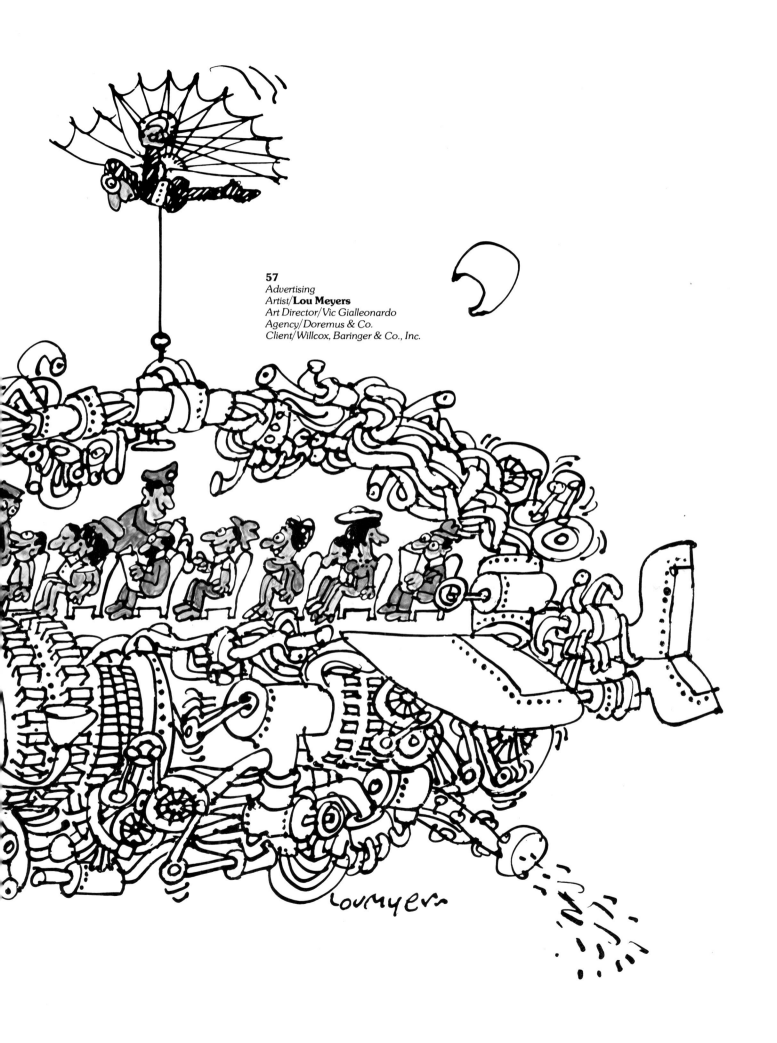

57
Advertising
*Artist/***Lou Meyers**
Art Director/Vic Gialleonardo
Agency/Doremus & Co.
Client/Willcox, Baringer & Co., Inc.

58
Editorial
*Artist/***Jim Sharpe**
Art Director/Joe Sapinsky
Publication/Woman's Day

59
Editorial
*Artist/***Daniel Schwartz**
Art Director/Daniel Schwartz

60
*Artist/***John Wallner**
Art Director/Margot Rechtiene & Virginia Copeland
Title/Flying Free
Publisher/McGraw-Hill Book Co.

61
Book
*Artist/***Miriam Schottland**
Art Director/Leonard Leone
Title/Stangers to Themselves
Publisher/Bantam Books, Inc.

62
Advertising
*Artist/***Etienne Delessert**
Art Director/A. Neal Siegel
Client/Smith, Kline & French Laboratories

63
Book
*Artist/***Leo Lionni**
Art Director/Janet Townsend
Title/The Greentail Mouse
Publisher/Random House, Inc.

64
Advertising
*Artist/***Judy Pelikan**
Art Director/Judy Pelikan
Client/Boston Educational Research

65
Editorial
*Artist/***Judith Hoffman Corwin**
Art Director/Jeanne Dzienciol
Publication/American Baby Magazine

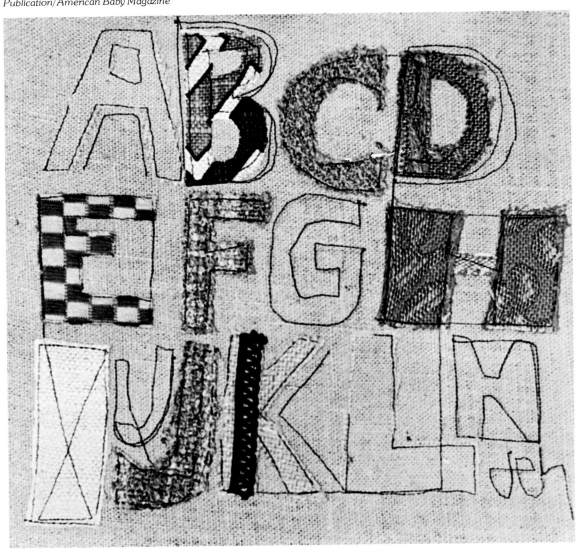

66
Film
*Artist/***Mike Kiernan & Bill Peckmann**
Art Director/Phil Kimmelman
Production/Phil Kimmelman & Associates, Inc.
Client/Dailey & Associates

67
Editorial
*Artist/***Barry Ross**
Art Director/Barry Ross

William Tell Overture

ugene Ormandy/The Philadelphia Orchestra

ntique; Järnefelt: Praeludium; Pierné: March of the Little Fauns; Kabalevsky: Comedian's Galop;
elibes: The Huntresses; Rimsky-Korsakov: Dance of the Tumblers; Saint-Saëns: Bacchanale

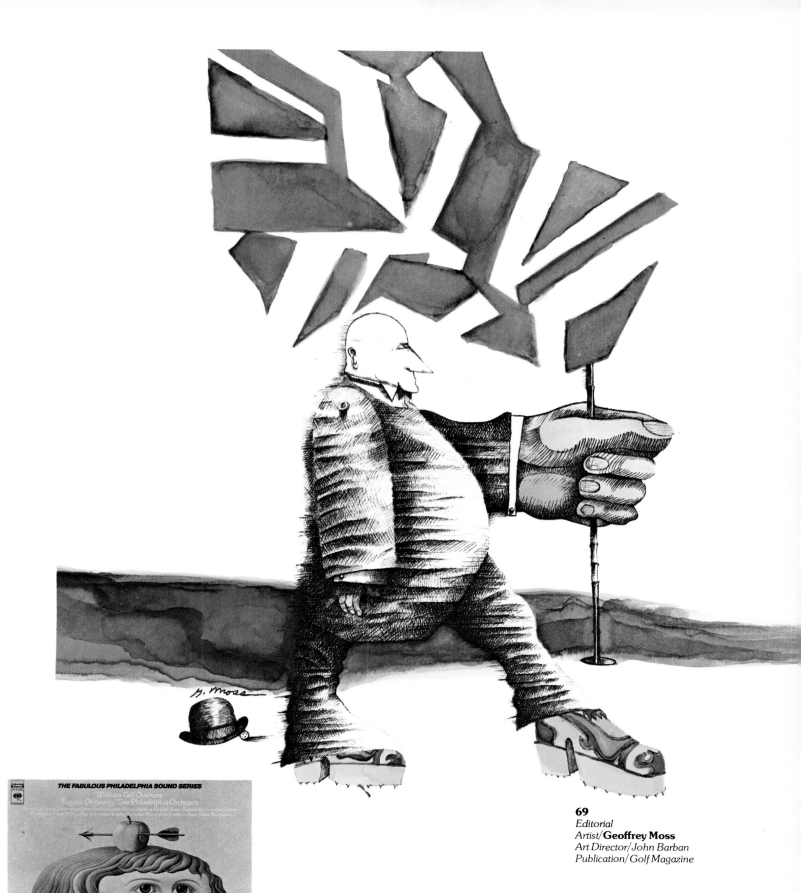

69
Editorial
*Artist/***Geoffrey Moss**
Art Director/John Barban
Publication/Golf Magazine

68
Advertising
*Artist/***Roy Carruthers**
Art Director/John Berg
Client/Columbia Records
Gold Medal

70
Advertising
*Artist/***David Levine**
Art Director/John Berg
Client/Columbia Records

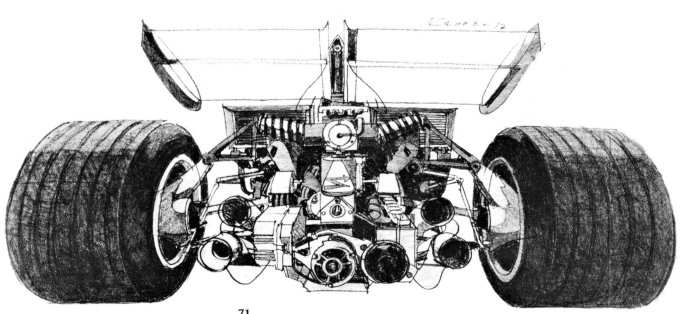

71
Advertising
*Artist/***Maurice Kennell**
Art Director/Kenny Schmid
Client/Firestone Rubber Co.

72 A,B,C,
Institutional
Artist/**John Schoenherr**
Art Director/Walter Miles
Client/National Audubon Society

73
Book
Artist/**Mark English**
Art Director/Barbara Bertoli
Title/No One Writes to the Colonel
Publisher/Avon Books

74
Book
Artist/**Joan Hall**
Art Director/Barbara Bertoli
Title/American Voices American Women
Publisher/Avon Books

75
Editorial
Artist/**Gerry Contreras**
Art Director/David Passalacqua
Publication/Genesis

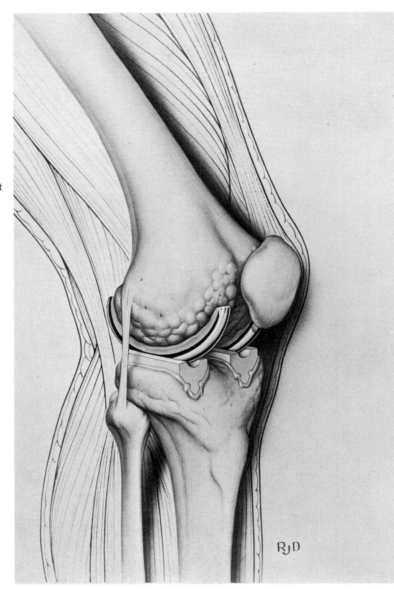

76
Advertising
Artist/**Robert J. Demarest**
Art Director/Richard Beck
Client/Eli Lilly & Co.

78
Editorial
Artist/**Norm MacDonald**
Art Director/Bud Loader
Publication/Flying Magazine

77
Book
Artist/**Leo & Diane Dillon**
Art Director/Tom Von Der Linn
Title/Gift of the Magi
Publisher/Reader's Digest Association

Life at Little Airports

79
Book
Artist/**Kenneth Francis Dewey**
Art Director/*David B. Rinne*

80
Editorial
Artist/**Richard A. Lopez**
Art Director/*Richard A. Lopez*

81
Advertising
Artist/**Norm Doherty**
Art Director/Frank Daniel
Client/Pickwick Records

82
Advertising
Artist/**Dennis Ziemienski**
Art Director/Steven Jacobs
Agency/Steven Jacobs Design, Inc.
Client/Simpson Lee Paper Co.

83
Advertising
*Artist/***Robert Andrew Parker**
Art Director/John Berg
Client/Columbia Records

84
Book
*Artist/***John Alcorn**
Art Director/Skip Sorvino
Title/Cook Up Tales
Publisher/Scholastic Magazines, Inc.

85
Book
*Artist/***Nita Engle**
Art Director/William Gregory
Title/The Years of the Forest
Publisher/Reader's Digest Association

86
Advertising
*Artist/***Harry Sehring**
Art Director/Harry Sehring
& Art Kaufman
Agency/William Douglas McAdams
Client/Roche Laboratories

87
Editorial
*Artist/***Dennis Lyall**
Art Director/Charles Thorp
Publication/Trans Ocean Annual Report

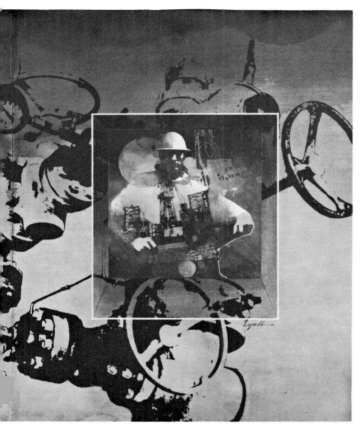

88
Book
*Artist/***Nita Engle**
Art Director/Marion Davis
Title/The Mountain Farm
Publisher/Reader's Digest Association

89
Film
*Artist/***Walter Einsel**
Art Director/Neil Tardio
Agency/Young & Rubicam, Inc.
Client/General Foods

90
Advertising
*Artist/***Cliff Condak**
Art Director/John Berg
Client/Columbia Records

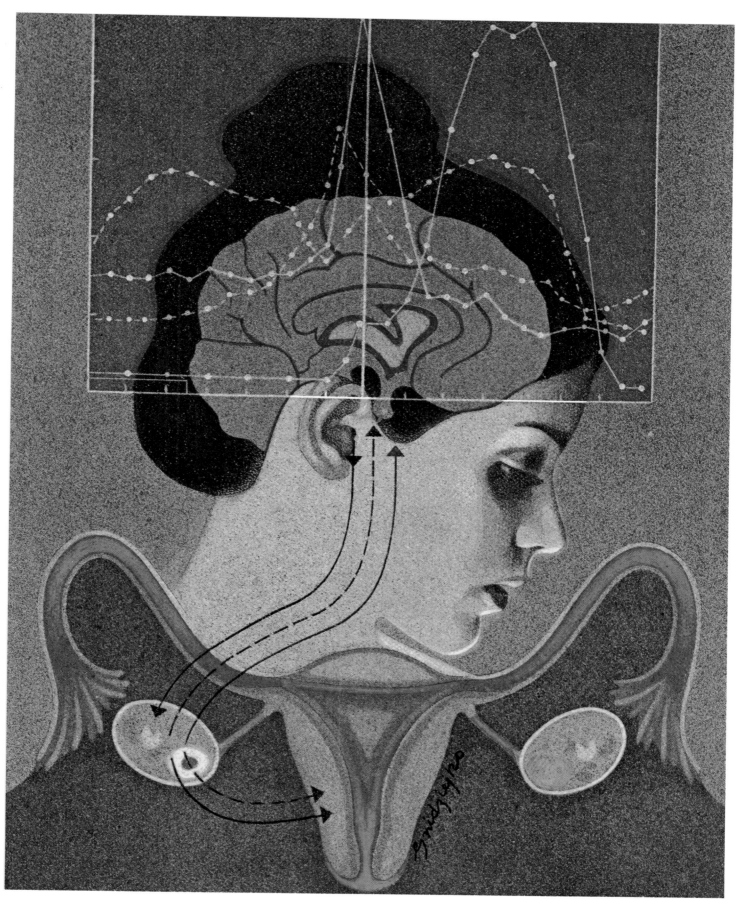

91
Artist/**Alex Gnidziejko**
Art Director/Arthur Beckenstein
Agency/Medcom, Inc.
Client/Wyeth Laboratories

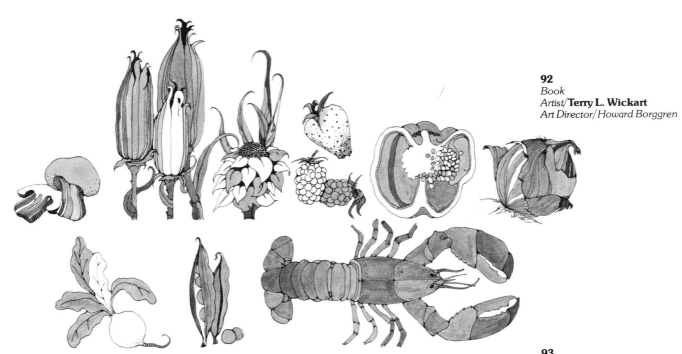

92
Book
*Artist/***Terry L. Wickart**
Art Director/Howard Borggren

93
Editorial
*Artist/***Jerry Pinkney**
Art Director/Nick Cruz & Bob Crozier
Publication/Boys' Life Magazine

94
Institutional
*Artist/***Pat Watkins**
Art Director/Pat Watkins

95
Editorial
*Artist/***Jerry Podwil**
Art Director/Arthur Paul
Publication/Playboy Magazine

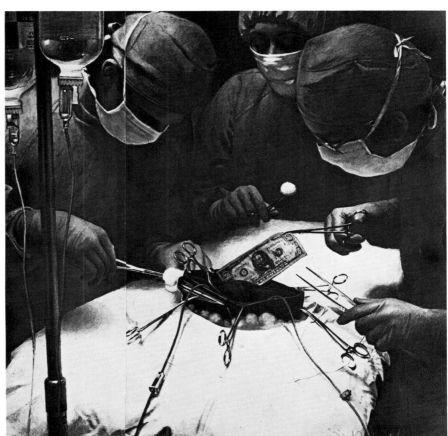

96
Book
*Artist/***Marty Norman**
Art Director/Lou Dorfsman
Title/A Seasonal Ailment Or…
Publisher/CBS Television Network

97
Book
Artist/**Jim Jonson**
Art Director/Jim Jonson
Title/Wrestlers
Publisher/Prentice-Hall, Inc.

99
Editorial
*Artist/***James Spanfeller**
Art Director/Robert Sadler
Publication/Mineral Digest

98
Advertising
*artist/***Charles White, III**
Art Director/John Berg
Client/Columbia Records

100
Book
*Artist/***David K. Stone**
Art Director/Al Cetta
Title/The Shadow of the Falcon

101
Institutional
*Artist/***Hiroko Tsuchihashi**
Art Director/Richard Wilde
Client/School of Visual Arts

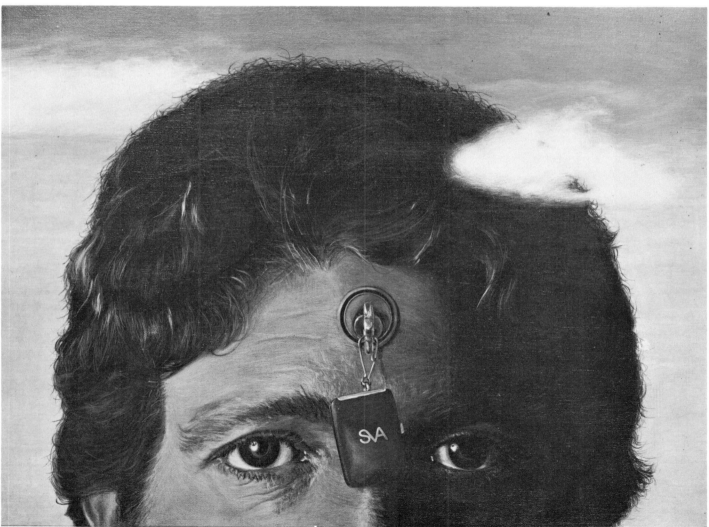

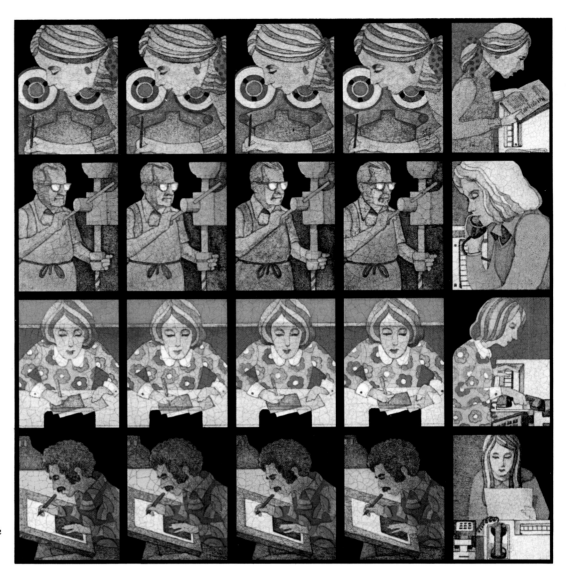

102
Institutional
Artist/**Jerry Cosgrove**
Art Director/John Vise
Client/Xerox Corp.

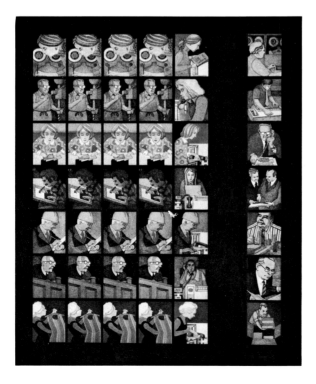

103
Editorial
Artist/**Doug Johnson**
Art Director/Jane Wilson
Publication/Viva Magazine

104
Advertising
*Artist/***John Buxton**
Art Director/Frederick E. Wallin
Agency/Frederick E. Wallin, Inc.
Client/European Health Spa

105
Institutional
*Artist/***Bart Forbes**
Art Director/Bart Forbes
Client/Brodnax Printing Co.

106
Advertising
*Artist/***Bernard Fuchs**
Art Director/Bernard Fuchs
Agency/Young & Rubicam, Inc.

107
Advertising
*Artist/***Don Ivan Punchatz**
Art Director/Barry Kaufman & Richard LoMonaco
Client/Avco Embassy Pictures

108
Book
*Artist/***Brad Holland**
Art Director/Frank Metz
Title/Governor Ramage
Publisher/Simon & Schuster, Inc.

109
Book
*Artist/***Bart Forbes**
Art Director/Charles Volpe
Title/The Silkie
Publisher/Ace Books

110
Editorial
*Artist/***Robert Heindel**
Art Director/Joe Sapinsky
Publication/Woman's Day

111
Editorial
*Artist/***Bernard Fuchs**
Art Director/Richard Ference
Publication/Golf Magazine
Gold Medal

112
Advertising
*Artist/***Delor Erickson**
Art Director/Nancy Rice
Agency/Knox Reeves Advertising
Client/West Publishing

113
Editorial
Artist/**Alice Brickner**
Art Director/Ken Hine
Publication/American Way Magazine

115
Book
Artist/**Sandy Kossin**
Art Director/Leonard Leone
Title/Macho!
Publisher/Bantam Books, Inc.

114
Book
Artist/**Nicholasa Mohr**
Art Director/*Anne Brown*
Title/*Nilda*
Publisher/*Harper & Row Publishers, Inc.*

116
Advertising
Artist/**Edward Jaciow**
Art Director/*Steve Jacobs*
Agency/*Steven Jacobs Design, Inc.*
Client/*White Stag Manufacturing Co., Inc.*

117
Editorial
Artist/**Bob McGinnis**
Art Director/*Bernard Springsteel*
Publication/*Good Housekeeping Magazine*

118
Book
*Artist/***Leo & Diane Dillon**
Art Director/Catherine Scar & Virginia Copeland
Title/Orange Rain
Publisher/Webster Division
      McGraw-Hill Book Co.

119
Book
*Artist/***Howard Koslow**
Art Director/Milton Charles
Title/Ocean World of Jacques Cousteau
Publisher/World Publishing Co.

120
Institutional
*Artist/***Robert Altemus**
Art Director/Robert Altemus
Client/U.S. Environmental Protection Agency

121
Institutional
*Artist/***Ignacio Gomez**
Art Director/John Anselmo
Client/Art Directors Club of Los Angeles

123
Advertising
Artist/**Guy Billout**
Art Director/Robert L. Heimall
Client/Elektra Records
Gold Medal

122
Advertising
Artist/**Albino Hinojosa**
Art Director/Albino Hinojosa

124
Institutional
*Artist/***Joe Ciardiello**
Art Director/Tony Vanderperk & Cipe Peneles
Client/Parsons School of Design

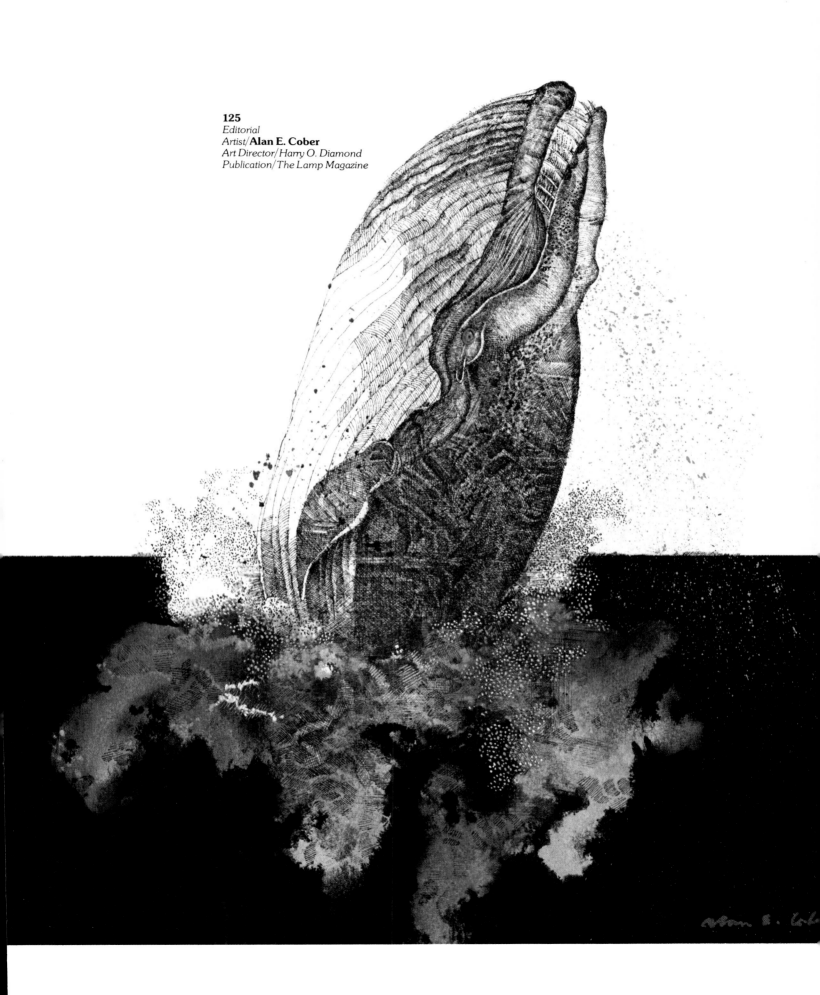

125
Editorial
*Artist/***Alan E. Cober**
Art Director/Harry O. Diamond
Publication/The Lamp Magazine

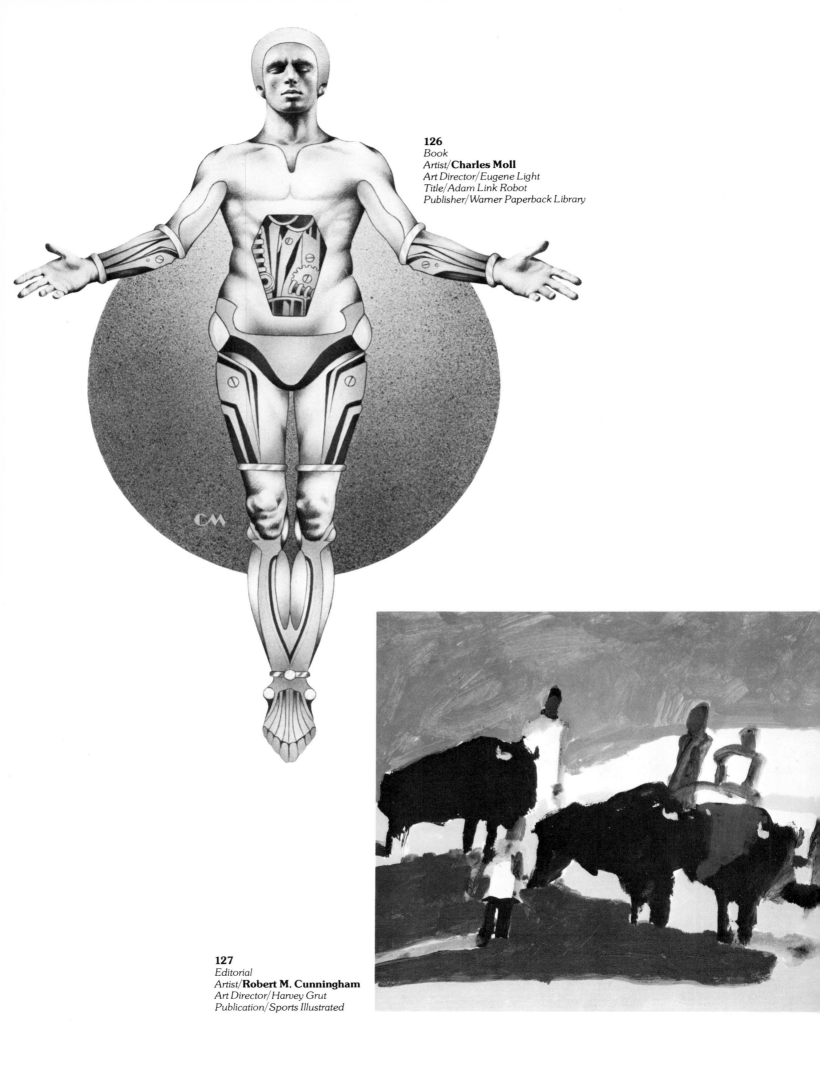

126
Book
*Artist/***Charles Moll**
Art Director/Eugene Light
Title/Adam Link Robot
Publisher/Warner Paperback Library

127
Editorial
*Artist/***Robert M. Cunningham**
Art Director/Harvey Grut
Publication/Sports Illustrated

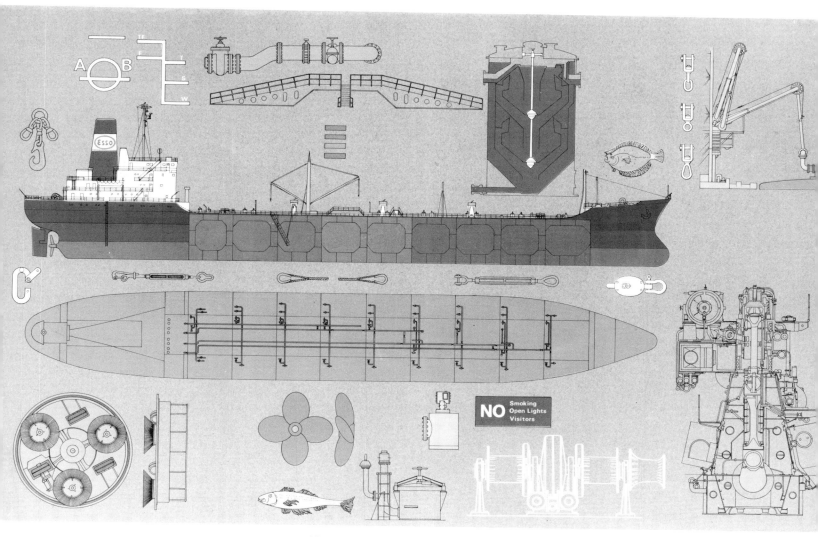

128
Editorial
Artist/**Tre Tryckare**
Art Director/Harry O. Diamond
Publication/The Lamp Magazine

129
Advertising
Artist/**Kyuzo Tsugami**
Art Director/Kyuzo Tsugami

130
Institutional
Artist/**Ignacio Gomez**
Art Director/Ron Wolin
Client/Art Directors Club of Los Angeles

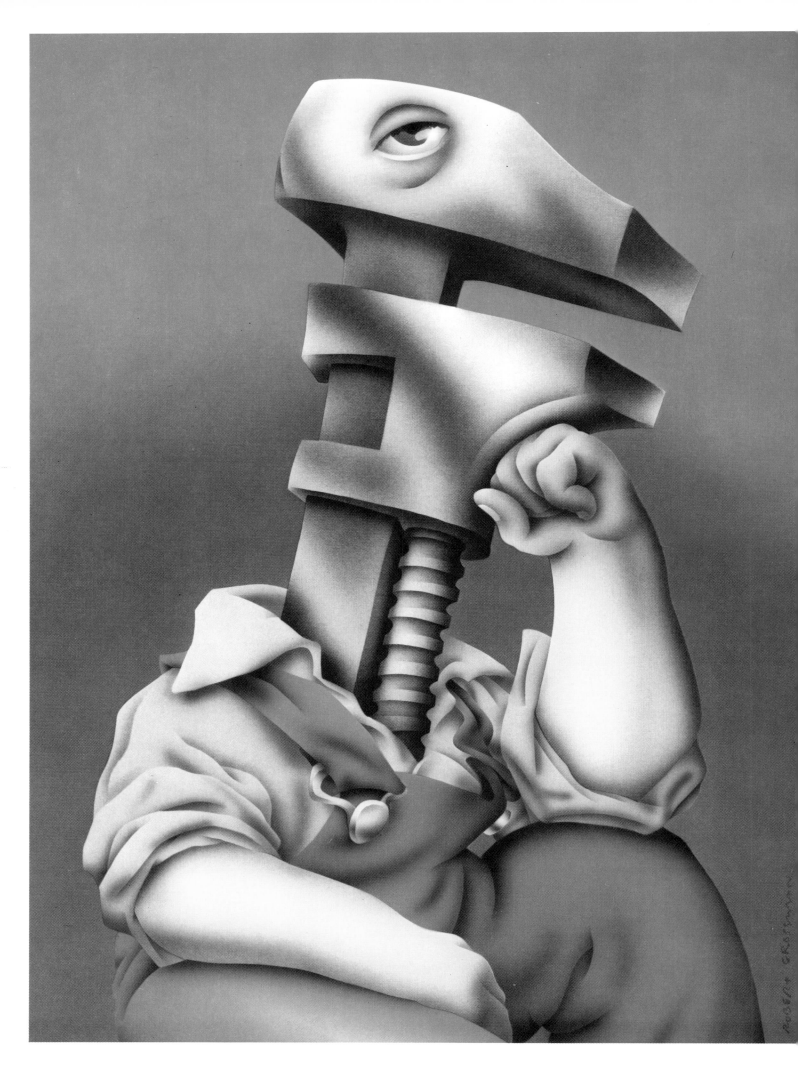

131
Editorial
*Artist/***Robert Grossman**
Art Director/David Olin
Publication/Signature Magazine

132
Editorial
*Artist/***Dennis Lyall**
Art Director/Alex Molinello
Publication/The Houston Post

133
Book
*Artist/***Ted CoConis**
Art Director/Edward Aho
Title/Apollo
Publisher/The Viking Press

134
Advertising
*Artist/***Lou Myers**
Art Director/Vic Gialleonardo & Vinnie Longo
Agency/Doremus & Co.
Client/Willcox, Baringer & Co., Inc.

135
Advertising
*Artist/***Paul Davis**
Art Director/Herb Lubalin
Agency/Lubalin, Smith, Carnase
Client/American Film Theatre

136
Advertising
Artist/**Jack Woolhiser**
Art Director/Gino Ingrassia
Agency/Prendergast-Walsh-Leventer, Inc.
Client/New Times Magazine

137
Institutional
Artist/**Larry Noble**
Art Director/Larry Noble
Client/Middaugh Associates, Inc.

138
Advertising
*Artist/***George S. Gaadt**
Art Director/Ron Blume
Agency/Pitt Studios
Client/Gallery Magazine

139
Institutional
*Artist/***Herbert Tauss**
Art Director/Herbert Tauss
Client/U.S. Department of the Interior

140
Book
*Artist/***Michael Eagle**
Art Director/Cynthia Basil
Title/The Curse of Laguna Grande
Publisher/Morrow Junior Books

141
Editorial
*Artist/***Herbert Tauss**
Art Director/Leo McCarthy
Publication/Penthouse Magazine

143
Book
Artist/**Ron Villani**
Art Director/*Will Gallagher*
Title/*Schizophrenia*
Publisher/*Encyclopaedia Britannica*

142
Book
Artist/**Ron Villani**
Art Director/*Will Gallagher*
Title/*Schizophrenia*
Publisher/*Encyclopaedia Britannica*

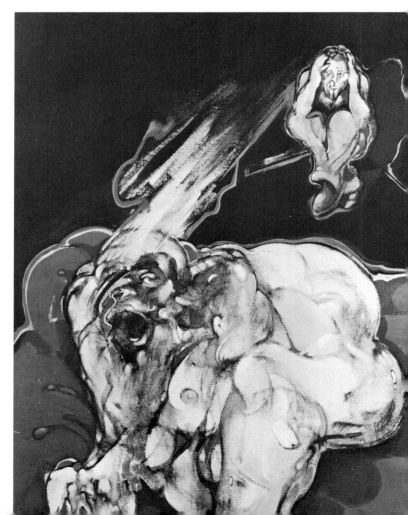

144
Book
Artist/**Ron Villani**
Art Director/*Will Gallagher*
Title/*Schizophrenia*
Publication/*Encyclopaedia Britannica*

145
Editorial
Artist/**Don Weller**
Art Director/Ray Yee
Publication/Flightime Magazine

147
Editorial
Artist/**Don Weller**
Art Director/Burnie Rotondo
Publication/PSA Magazine

146
Editorial
Artist/**Don Weller**
Art Director/Elin Waite
Publication/Westways Magazine

148
Advertising
*Artist/***David A. Leffel**
Art Director/Bob Ciano
Client/CTI Records

149
Advertising
*Artist/***Murray Tinkelman & James Spanfeller**
& Shelley Sacks
Art Director/Joel Siegel
Client/Hydra

150
Institutional
Artist/**David Kilmer**
Art Director/Ramon Orellana
Client/Grant Jacoby, Inc.

152
Book
Artist/**David Palladini**
Art Director/Sallie Baldwin
Title/Myself I Must Remake
Publisher/Thomas Y. Crowell Co.

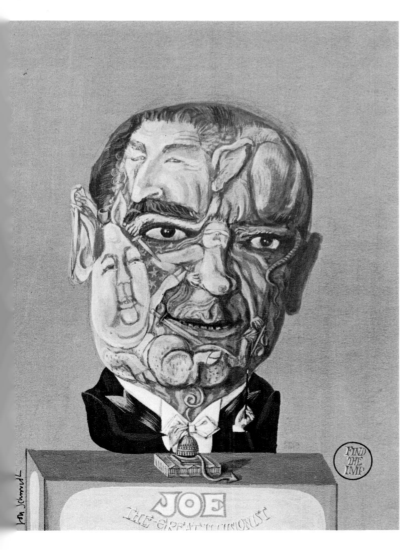

151
Advertising
Artist/**Eric Von Schmidt**
Art Director/Don Owens

153
Advertising
*Artist/***Gene Szafran**
Art Director/Gene Szafran

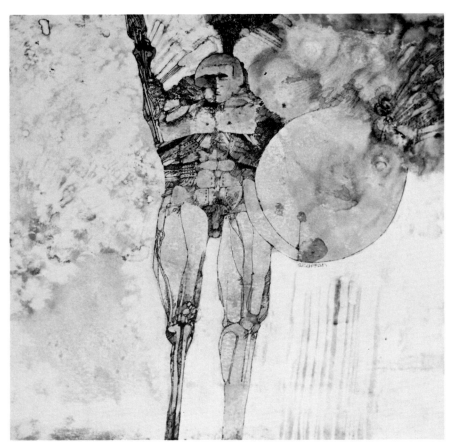

154
Advertising
*Artist/***Susan Obrant**
Art Director/John Davidson
Client/Orphic Egg—London Records

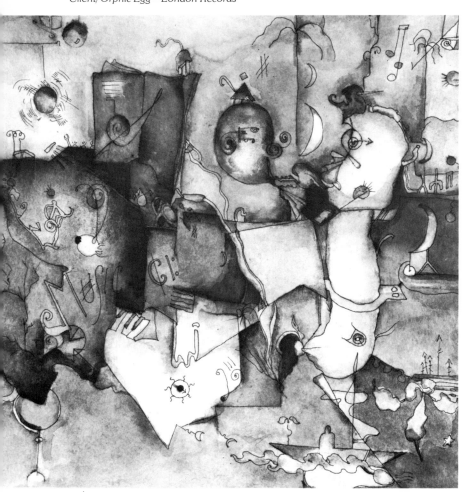

156
Advertising
Artist/ **Gene Szafran**
Art Director/Gene Szafran

157
Editorial
Artist/ **Al Bates**
Art Director/Al Bates
Publication/The Houston Clubber

155
Book
Artist/ **Robert LoGrippo**
Art Director/Robert LoGrippo

158
Institutional
*Artist/***Donald V. Crowley**
Art Director/Bob Hayes
Agency/Echelon Publishing
Client/Boys Clubs of America

159
Institutional
*Artist/***Eugene Tulley**
Art Director/Bill Harkins
Agency/Grant-Jacoby, Inc.

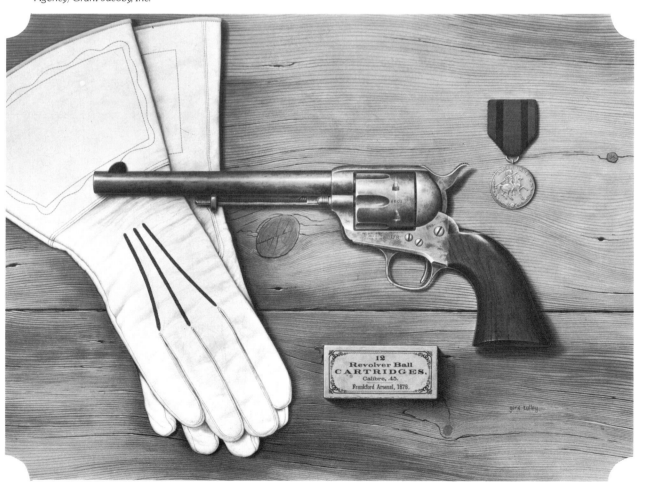

160
Institutional
*Artist/***Henry Kolodziej**
Art Director/Gary Shortt
Client/McNamara Associates

162
Advertising
*Artist/***Gilbert L. Stone**
Art Director/Silas Rhodes
Client/School of Visual Arts

161
Editorial
*Artist/***David B. Patrick**
Art Director/Robert Jensen

163
Editorial
*Artist/***Brad Holland**
Art Director/Arthur Paul
Publication/Playboy Magazine

164
Book
*Artist/***Don Ivan Punchatz**
Art Director/James Plumeri
Title/The Lucifer Society
Publisher/New American Library

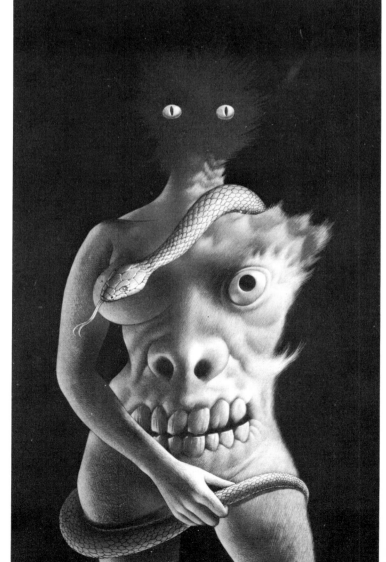

165
Advertising
*Artist/***James Ceribello**
Art Director/Leonard Kabatsky
Client/Volitant Publishing Co.

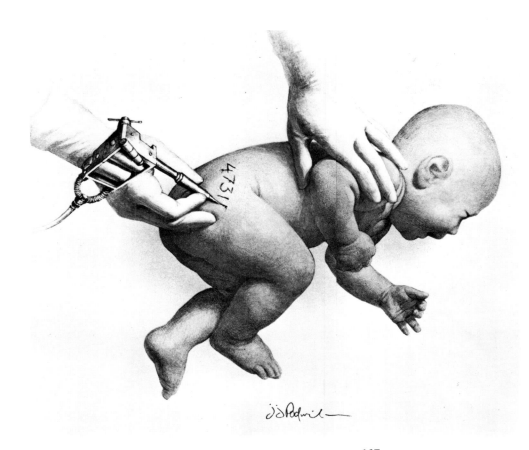

167
Editorial
*Artist/***Jerry Podwil**
Art Director/Arthur Paul
Publication/Playboy Magazine

166
Advertising
*Artist/***Fred Nelson**
Art Director/Fred Nelson

169
Book
*Artist/***Ben Stahl**
Art Director/James K. Davis
Title/A Pocketful of Seeds
Publisher/Doubleday & Co., Inc.

168
Institutional
*Artist/***Charles Santore**
Art Director/Elmer Pizzi
Agency/Gray & Rogers, Inc.
Client/Weyerhaeuser (Paper Division)

170
Advertising
*Artist/***Cliff Condak**
Art Director/John Berg
Client/Columbia Records

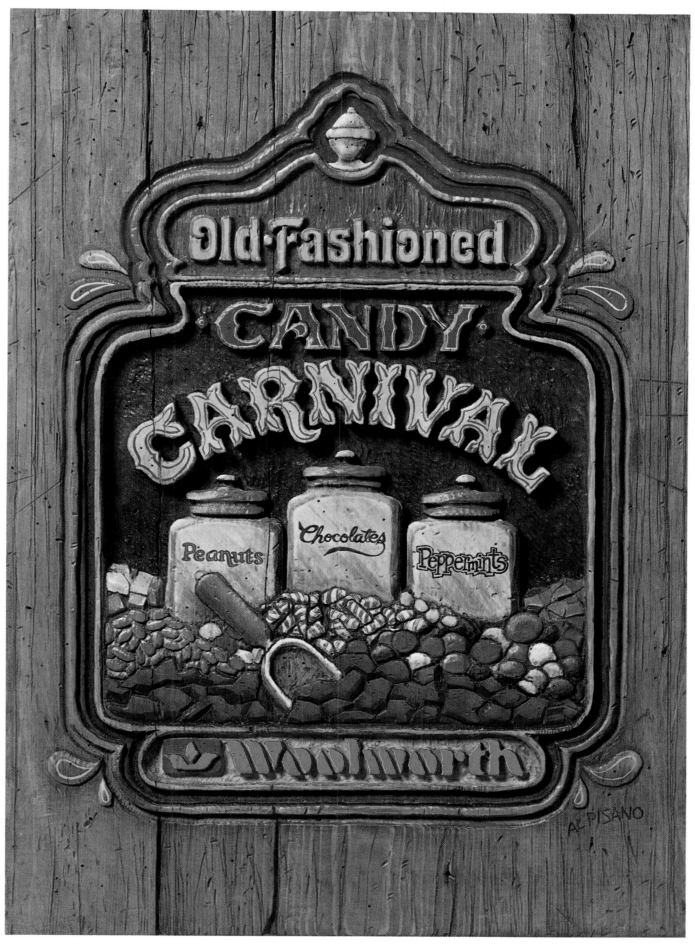

171
Advertising
*Artist/**Al Pisano***
Art Director/Charles McMains
Client/F. W. Woolworth Co.

174
Institutional
*Artist/***Robert Peak**
Art Director/Robert Peak

175
Film
*Artist/***Arthur Eckstein**
Art Director/Lou Dorfsman
Producer/Carnig Ermoyan
Production/Dolphin Productions
Client/WCAU-TV

176
Book
*Artist/***Elias Dominguez**
Art Director/Lidia Ferrara
Title/The Counterfeiters
Publisher/Random House, Inc.

177
Advertising
*Artist/***David K. Stone**
Art Director/Frank Daniel
Client/Pickwick Records

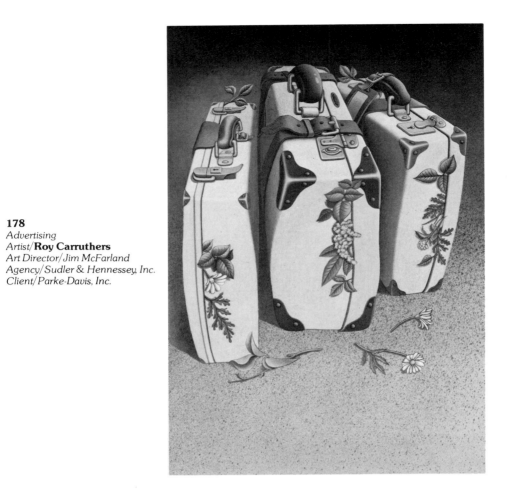

178
Advertising
*Artist/***Roy Carruthers**
Art Director/Jim McFarland
Agency/Sudler & Hennessey, Inc.
Client/Parke-Davis, Inc.

179
Advertising
*Artist/***David Wilcox**
Art Director/Jim McFarland
Agency/Sudler & Hennessey, Inc.
Client/Parke-Davis, Inc.

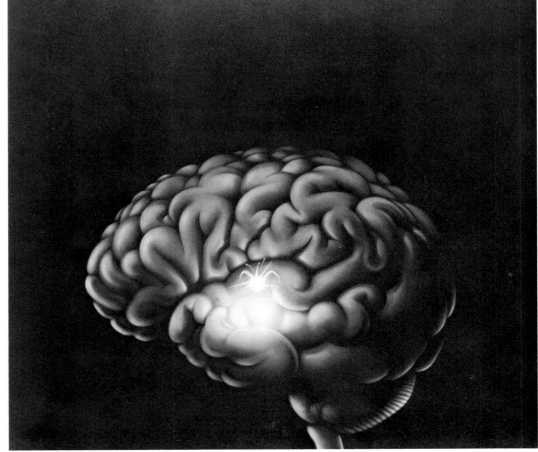

180
Editorial
*Artist/***Ignacio Gomez**
Art Director/Mike Brock
Publication/Oui Magazine

181
Advertising
*Artist/***Gary Overacre**
Art Director/Gary Overacre

182
Institutional
*Artist/***Eugene Karlin**
Art Director/John deCesare
Client/Geigy Pharmaceuticals

183
Editorial
*Artist/***Guy Billout**
Art Director/Paul Hardy
Publication/Super 8 Magazine
Gold Medal

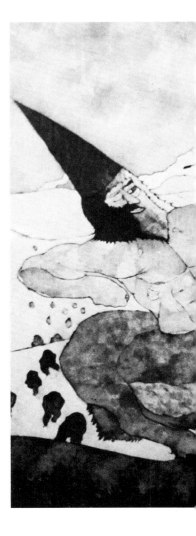

184
Advertising
*Artist/***Bruce Wolfe**
Art Director/Bruce Wolfe
Client/Professional Color Lab

185
Book
Artist/**Frank Bozzo**
Art Director/*Susan Mann*
Title/*Impossible People*
Publisher/*Holt, Rinehart & Winston, Inc.*

186
Institutional
Artist/**Gervasio Gallardo**
Art Director/*Gervasio Gallardo*
Award of Excellence

187
Advertising
Artist/**Ted CoConis**
Art Director/*Acy Lehman & Joe Stelmach*
Client/*RCA Records*

189
Advertising
*Artist/***Fred Otnes**
Art Director/Alex Vella
Client/American Express

188
Institutional
*Artist/***Mark English**
Art Director/Elmer Pizzi
Agency/Gray & Rogers
Client/Weyerhaeuser (Paper Division)
Award of Excellence

His beard rippled pretty in the wind
as he got set to fly his kite.
He ran down the hill
and caught the updraft in his kite.
He let go, she dipped,
he played out string, and up she sailed.
Uncle John's kite was on the wind!
Through the string in his hand
he could feel the kite
tugging and pulling away, eager to fly.
Easy, he let out the string,
smooth as silk.

But Reuben Robin was bound-determined
to have that string,
the very best
nest-building string he'd seen,
smooth as silk and strong as steel.
Swooping and screeching,
he followed Kite Uncle John up the hill,
tree branch to fence post,
scolding all the way,
telling the old man
what a rotten homebreaker he was.
He didn't know the meaning of fear,
that robin.
He just wanted Uncle John's string.
Kite Uncle John
didn't yell at the bird, though.
He was a patient man,
and he figured the robin
would give up and go away.

190A, B, C
Book
*Artist/***Janet McCaffery**
Art Director/Cynthia Basil
Title/The Battle of Reuben Robin & Kite Uncle John
Publisher/Morrow Junior Books

He shinnied up the tree,
with the robins flapping around his ears,
squawking.
"I'll just unravel your nest, Reuben!"
he said to that fat man robin.
"Teach you to go a-thieving!"
Laughing, he pulled his kite string
down from the nest.
Mad?
Say, that Reuben Robin screeched up a clack
like Uncle John had stolen
his first-born son!
That hot-headed robin hopped and squawked
and flew in to nip at the string.
Kite Uncle John
only brushed him off patiently,
got his kite from the back porch,
and set off for his kite-flying hill.

191
Book
*Artist/***Gene Szafran**
Art Director/Gene Szafran

192
Book
*Artist/***Tony Chen**
Art Director/Tony DeLuna
Title/Honnschi the Chicadee
Publisher/Parents' Magazine Press

By 1999, telephone service in America's biggest cities may catch up to Ironton, Pennsylvania.

193
Advertising
*Artist/***Frank Bozzo**
Art Director/George Lambos
Agency/Young & Rubicam, Inc.
Client/Stromberg Carlson

194
Editorial
*Artist/***Don Ivan Punchatz**
Art Director/John Davis & Don Menell
Publisher/Oui Magazine

195
Book
*Artist/***Ronald A. Recchio**
Art Director/Ronald A. Recchio

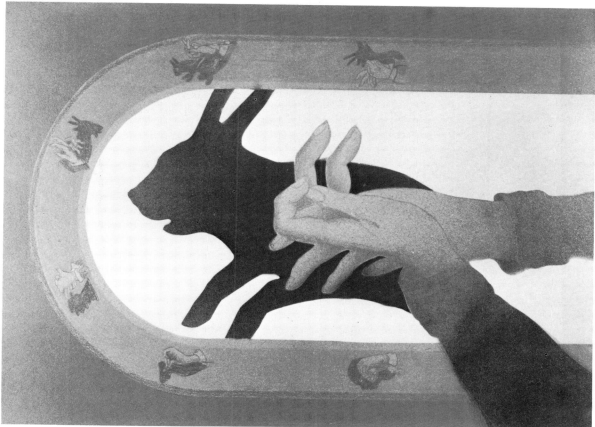

197
Advertising
*Artist/***Gary & Mary Schenck**
Art Director/Gary Schenck

196
Editorial
*Artist/***Walter Einsel**
Art Director/Harry Redler
Publication/Connecticut Magazine

198
Film
*Artist/***Harvey Kurtzman**
Art Director/Phil Kimmelman
Agency/Phil Kimmelman & Associates, Inc.
Client/Children's TV Workshop

199
Film
*Artist/***Tom Yohe**
Art Director/Tom Yohe
Agency/McCaffrey & McCall, Inc.
Client/ABC-TV

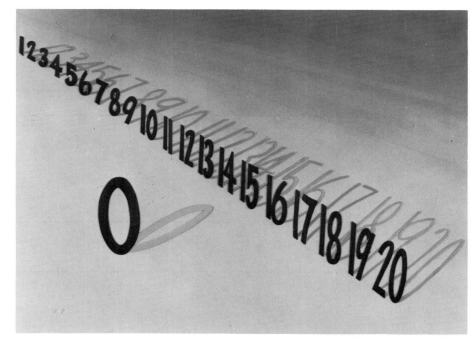

200
Film
*Artist/***Harvey Kurtzman**
Art Director/Phil Kimmelman
Agency/Phil Kimmelman & Associates, Inc.
Client/Children's TV Workshop

201
Book
Artist/**Paul L. Taylor**
Art Director/Paul L. Taylor
Title/Backward Beasts
Publisher/Bowmar Publishing Corp.

202
Advertising
Artist/**Lois Strasberg**
Art Director/Lois Strasberg
Agency/Evolution Records
Client/Stereo Dimensions, Inc.

203
Book
Artist/**Bruce Barkley**
Art Director/Bruce Barkley

204
Advertising
Artist/**Bobbye Cochran**
Art Director/Bobbye Cochran
Client/Falstaff Brewing Co.

205
Book
Artist/**Bob Jones**
Art Director/Bob Jones

207
Institutional
*Artist/***Richard Hess**
Art Director/Ed Chason
Agency/Producer's Row
Client/Xerox Corp.

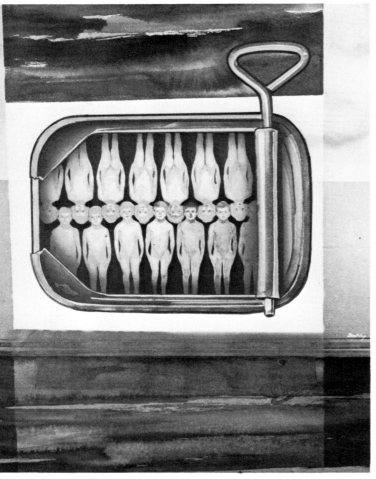

206
Advertising
*Artist/***James Barkley**
Art Director/Dick Bennett
Client/NBC Television

208
Editorial
*Artist/***Carol Anthony**
Art Director/Stan Mack
Publication/The New York Times

209
Book
*Artist/***Arthur Lidov**
Art Director/Leonard Leone
Title/Self-Image Surgery
Publisher/Bantam Books, Inc.
Award of Excellence

210
Advertising
*Artist/***James Barkley**
Art Director/Dick Bennett
Client/NBC Television

212
Book
*Artist/***Cathy Porter**
Art Director/Cathy Porter

211
Editorial
*Artist/***George Sottung**
Art Director/George Sottung

213
Institutional
*Artist/***Karl W. Swanson**
Art Director/Karl W. Swanson

214
Institutional
*Artist/***Karl W. Swanson**
Art Director/Karl W. Swanson

215
Institutional
*Artist/***Gene Hoffman**
Art Director/Gene Hoffman

216
Institutional
*Artist/***Gene Hoffman**
Art Director/Gene Hoffman
Client/Dixon Paper Co.

217
Book
*Artist/***Bob McGinnis**
Art Director/Leonard Leone
Title/No More Dying Then
Publisher/Bantam Books, Inc.

218
Advertising
*Artist/***Judy McGuggart**
Art Director/Walter Kaprielian
Agency/Ketchum, MacLeod & Grove, Inc.
Client/Newark District Ford Dealers

219
Book
*Artist/***David Kilmer**
Art Director/David Kilmer

220
Institutional
*Artist/***Sandy Huffaker**
Art Director/Sandy Huffaker
Client/Pema Browne

221
Book
*Artist/***Hal Ashmead**
Art Director/(Mrs.) Riki Levinson
Title/Trouble at Second
Publisher/E. P. Dutton & Co., Inc.

222
Editorial
*Artist/***Randall Enos**
Art Director/Stan Braverman
Publication/Tennis Magazine

223
Book
*Artist/***Frank Marciuliano**
Art Director/Jerry Leff

224
Institutional
*Artist/***Robert Peak**
Art Director/Martin Stevens
Agency/Harvey Kahn Associates
Client/Living Legends, Ltd.
Award of Excellence

225
Editorial
*Artist/***John F. Dyess**
Art Director/John F. Dyess

227
Advertising
*Artist/***Howard Terpning**
Art Director/Jack Marinelli
Client/Winchester—Western

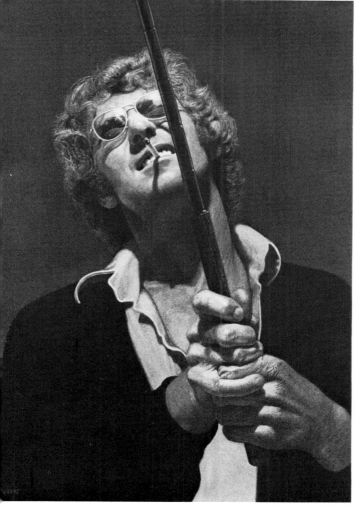

226
Editorial
*Artist/***Peter Swan**
Art Director/Jonathan Eby
Publication/Quest

229
Institutional
*Artist/***Gerald McConnell**
Art Director/Gerald McConnell

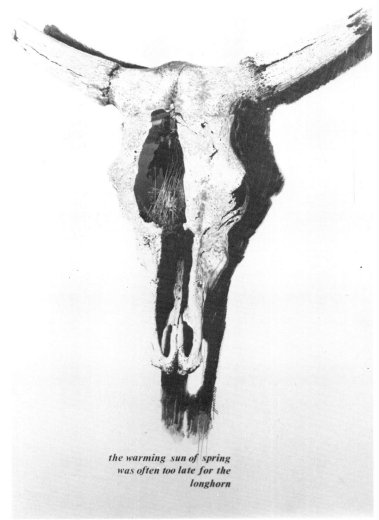

*the warming sun of spring
was often too late for the
longhorn*

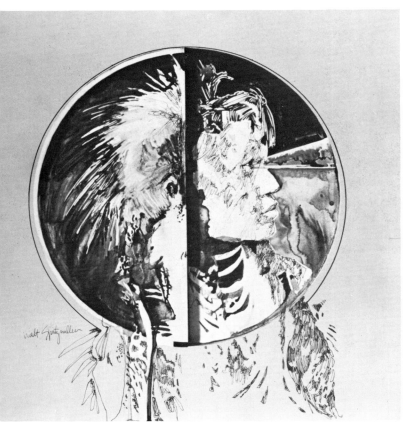

228
Advertising
*Artist/***Walter Spitzmiller**
Art Director/Walter Spitzmiller

230
Book
*Artist/***Arvis L. Stewart**
Art Director/Arvis L. Stewart
Publisher/Houghton Mifflin Co.

231
Book
*Artist/***Robert Heindel**
Art Director/James Plumeri
Title/American Epic
Publisher/New American Library
Award of Excellence

232
Book
*Artist/***Arvis L. Stewart**
Art Director/Arvis L. Stewart
Publisher/Houghton Mifflin Co.

233
Book
*Artist/***Ted Michener**
Art Director/Ted Michener

234
Book
*Artist/***Charles Mikolaycak**
Art Director/Linda Zuckerman
Title/Forerunner Foray
Publisher/Viking Press, Inc.

235
Institutional
*Artist/***Richard S. Terrell**
Art Director/Richard S. Terrell

236
Institutional
*Artist/***Jerry Pinkney**
Art Director/Elmer Pizzi
Agency/Gray & Rogers, Inc.
Client/Weyerhaeuser (Paper Division)

237
Advertising
*Artist/***Roy Carruthers**
Art Director/Jim McFarland
Agency/Sudler & Hennessey, Inc.
Client/Parke-Davis, Inc.

238
Editorial
*Artist/***David Grove**
Art Director/David Grove
Publication/California Living Magazine

239
Editorial
*Artist/***Norman Green**
Art Director/Jane Wilson
Publication/Seventeen Magazine

241
Advertising
*Artist/***Carole Jean (Feuerman)**
Art Director/Frank Valentino & Rocco Russo
Client/Lyrical Image, Inc.

240
Book
*Artist/***David Grove**
Art Director/John Cavalla
Title/Civil War III
Publisher/Field Educational Publishers, Inc.

243
Institutional
*Artist/***Hugh McMahon**
Art Director/Hugh McMahon

242
Advertising
*Artist/***Edward Sorel**
Art Director/John Berg
Client/Columbia Records

244
Book
*Artist/***Gerry Contreras**
Art Director/Tom Von Der Linn
Title/Witness for the Prosecution
Publisher/Reader's Digest Association

245
Editorial
*Artist/***Kenneth Francis Dewey**
Art Director/Dale Moyer
Publication/Scholastic Magazine

246
Book
*Artist/***Marshall Arisman**
Art Director/Richard Wilde
Title/Frozen Images
Publisher/Visual Arts Press

247
Institutional
*Artist/***Chris Spollen**
Art Director/Bernard D'Andrea
& Cipe Pineles
Client/Parsons School of Design

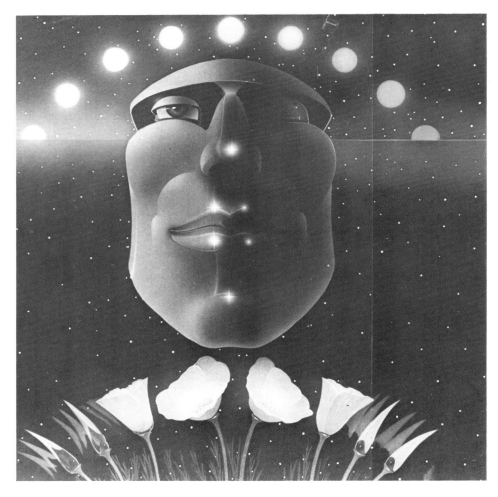

248
Book
*Artist/***Peter Lloyd**
Art Director/Will Gallagher
Title/The Clocks Within Us
Publisher/Encyclopaedia Britannica

249
Editorial
*Artist/***Kathy Calderwood**
Art Director/Arthur Paul
Publication/Playboy Magazine

251
Institutional
*Artist/***Richard Hess**
Art Director/Ed Chason
Agency/Producer's Row
Client/Xerox Corp.

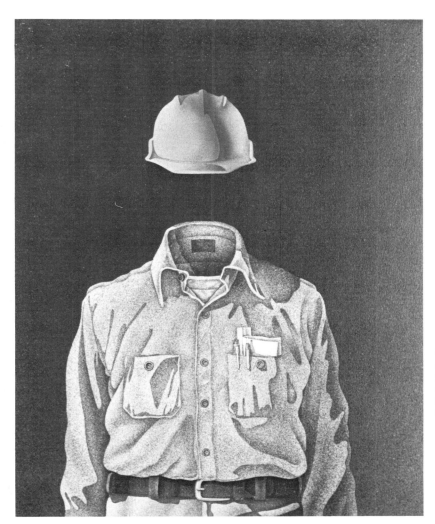

250
Advertising
*Artist/***David M. Gaadt**
Art Director/Preuit Holland
Agency/Cargill, Wilson & Acree
Client/Alabama Power Co.

252
Advertising
Artist/**Doug Johnson**
Art Director/Michael David
Client/Chelsea Theatre

253
Film
Artist/**John Sovjani**
Art Director/Dolores Gudzin
Client/NBC

254
Advertising
*Artist/***Paul Williams**
Art Director/Paul Williams

256
Advertising
*Artist/***Doug Johnson**
Art Director/Mike Salisbury
Client/United Artists Records

255
Institutional
*Artist/***Jerry Pinkney**
Art Director/Jeff Rapalae
Agency/Frederick Siebel Associates
Client/Seagram

257
Book
*Artist/***Jeffrey W. Cornell**
Art Director/Jeffrey W. Cornell

258
Institutional
*Artist/***Christine Duke**
Art Director/Christine Duke

259
Editorial
Artist/**Daniel Schwartz**
Art Director/Alvin Grossman & Modesto Torre
Publication/McCall's Magazine

260
Editorial
Artist/**Paul Giovanopoulos**
Art Director/Stan Mack
Publication/The New York Times

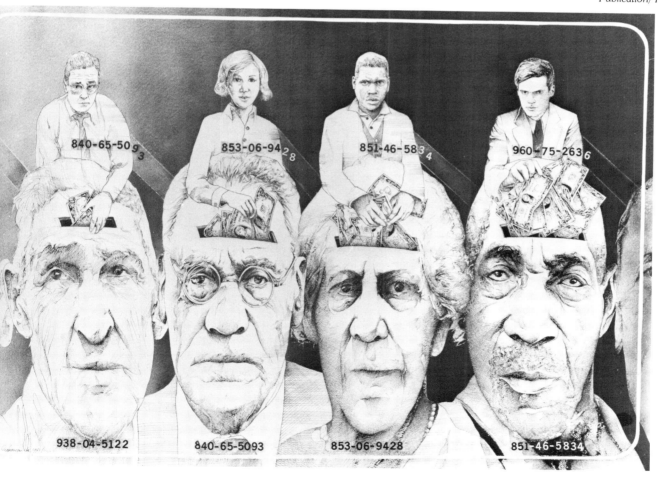

262
Editorial
Artist/**Edward Soyka**
Art Director/Randee Rubin
Publication/Medical Dimensions Magazine

261
Institutional
Artist/**James Ceribello**
Art Director/James Ceribello
Agency/Fat Cat Studio
Client/James Ceribello

263
Advertising
Artist/**David Wilcox**
Art Director/Jim McFarland
Agency/Sudler & Hennessey, Inc.
Client/Parke-Davis, Inc.

264
Book
*Artist/*__Fred Pfeiffer__
Art Director/Leonard Leone
Title/The Sword of the Golem
Publisher/Bantam Books, Inc.

265
Institutional
*Artist/*__Paul Giovanopoulos__
Art Director/Paul Giovanopoulos
Client/Annette Kossen

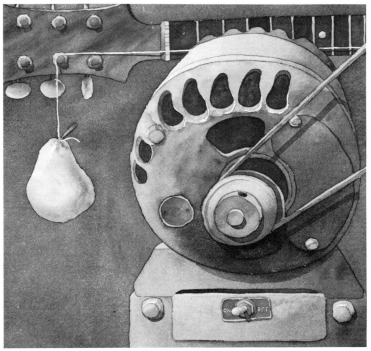

266
Institutional
*Artist/***Richard Egielski**
Art Director/Bernard D'Andrea & Cipe Pineles
Client/Parsons School of Design

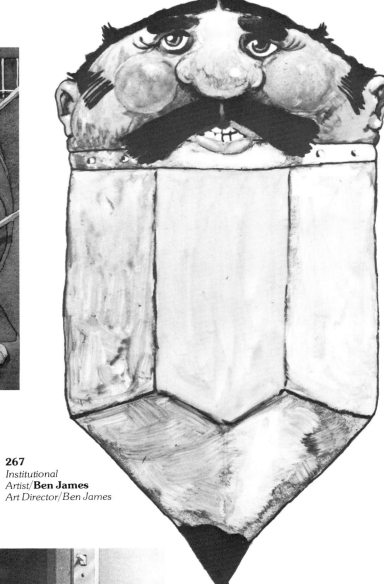

267
Institutional
*Artist/***Ben James**
Art Director/Ben James

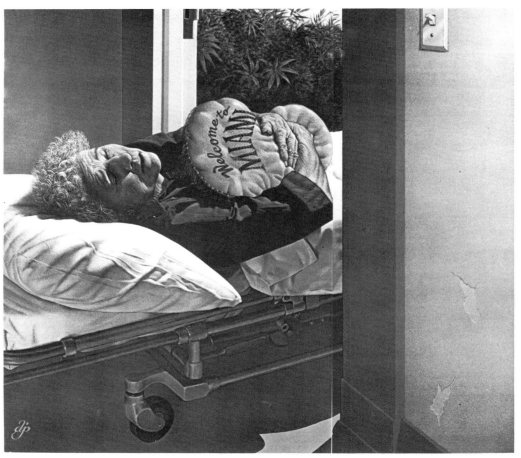

268
Editorial
*Artist/***Don Ivan Punchatz**
Art Director/Arthur Paul
Publication/Playboy Magazine

269
Advertising
*Artist/**Robert Andrew Parker***
Art Director/John Berg
Client/Columbia Records

270
Advertising
*Artist/***Rick Brown**
Art Director/Alan J. Klawans
Client/Smith, Kline & French Laboratories

271
Book
*Artist/***Mercer Mayer**
Art Director/Mildred Kantrowitz & Tony DeLuna
Title/While the Horses Galloped to London
Publisher/Parents' Magazine Press

272
Advertising
*Artist/***Gary Solin**
Art Director/Andrew Kner
Agency/Inter/Graph Ltd.
Client/The New York Times

273
Advertising
*Artist/***Kyuzo Tsugami**
Art Director/Kyuzo Tsugami

274
Book
Artist/**Norman Laliberté**
Art Director/Sallie Baldwin
Title/The Castle of Ladies
Publisher/Thomas Y. Crowell Co.

The Castle of Ladies

Retold by Constance Hieatt

Illustrated by Norman Laliberté

275
Book
*Artist/***Tony Chen**
Art Director/Leslie Bauman
Publisher/Holt, Rinehart & Winston, Inc.

276
Advertising
*Artist/**Andrew Wages***
Art Director/Dick Boone
Agency/The Stamford Agency
Client/The Southland Corp.

277
Book
*Artist/**William Edwards***
Art Director/Leonard Leone
Title/The Golden Notebook
Publisher/Bantam Books, Inc.

278
Editorial
*Artist/**Robert A. Weaver***
Art Director/Stan Mack
Publication/The New York Times

279
Book
*Artist/***Howard Rogers**
Art Director/Leonard Leone
Title/The Original
Publisher/Bantam Books, Inc.

281
Advertising
*Artist/***Nick Aristovulos**
Art Director/Norm Schaefer
Client/Intellectual Digest

280
Editorial
*Artist/***Lorraine Fox**
Art Director/Joan Fenton
Publication/Seventeen Magazine

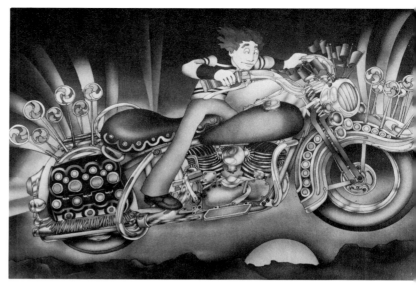

282
Book
*Artist/***Michael Horen**
Art Director/Judie Mills
Title/The Neon Motorcycle
Publisher/Franklin Watts, Inc.

albino Hinojosa 72

283
Advertising
*Artist/***Hedda**
Art Director/Herb Lubalin
Agency/Lubalin, Smith, Carnase, Inc.
Client/American Film Theatre

284
Advertising
*Artist/***Albino Hinojosa**
Art Director/Albino Hinojosa
Client/Uniquities

285
Advertising
*Artist/***David M. Gaadt**
Art Director/David M. Gaadt
Client/Michael Parver Associates

286
Editorial
*Artist/***James Spanfeller**
Art Director/Ira Silberlicht
Publication/Emergency Medicine

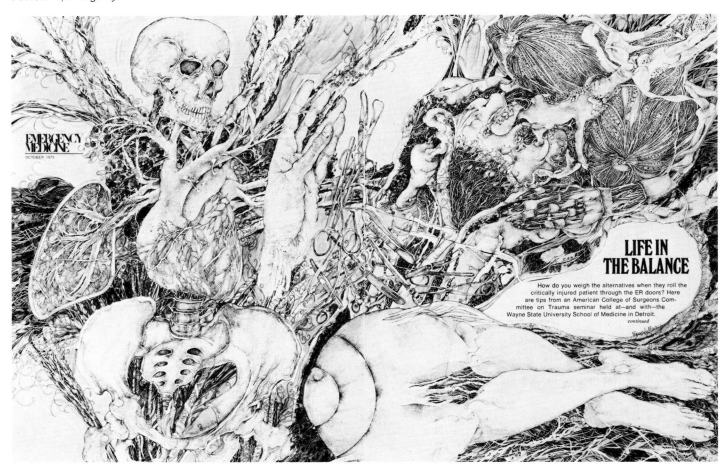

287
Editorial
*Artist/***Michael Eagle**
Art Director/Nye Wilden
Publication/Cavalier Magazine

288
Book
*Artist/***David McCall Johnston**
Art Director/Barbara Bertoli
Title/Summering
Publisher/Avon Books

289
Advertising
*Artist/***Steve Karchin**
Art Director/Werner Pfeiffer
Client/Repertory Theatre of Lincoln Center

290
Book
Artist/**Brad Holland**
Art Director/Frank Metz
Title/Gower Street
Publisher/Simon & Schuster, Inc.
Gold Medal

ER STREET
ovel by Claire Rayner

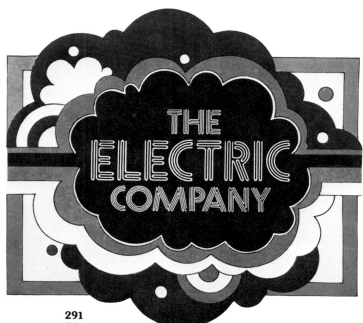

291
Film
Artist/**Bob Blansky**
Art Director/Bob Blansky
Producer/Carnig Ermoyan
Production/Dolphin Productions
Client/Children's TV Workshop

292
Editorial
Artist/**Tom Haygood**
Art Director/Tom Haygood
Publication/Titan

293
Institutional
*Artist/***Ed Lindlof**
Art Director/Gary Bunch
Agency/Goodwin, Dannenbaum, Littman &
Wingfield, Inc.
Client/Capital National Corp.

294
Book
*Artist/***Bob Brown**
Art Director/June Davis
Title/Today
Publisher/Prentice-Hall, Inc.

295
Editorial
*Artist/***Alex Ebel**
Art Director/Norman S. Hotz
Publication/Travel & Leisure

296
Advertising
*Artist/***Don Wieland & Jerry Cosgrove**
Art Director/Helmut Krone
Agency/Doyle Dane Bernbach, Inc.
Client/Audi-Fox

A Fox is quick (0 to 50 in 10 seconds).
It's surefooted (front-wheel drive).
This sly, cunning sedan can take the
sharpest turns nimbly (sports car type
steering and suspension). It can
stop practically in its tracks
(power front disc brakes). And it doesn't
eat much (23 miles per gallon).
Best of all, for under $3,200*you
can catch the Fox.

YOUR HUNT IS OVER. THE QUICK, SLY, CRAFTY, CUNNING FOX BY AUDI IS HERE.

298
Institutional
*Artist/***Rose Farber**
Art Director/Rose Farber
Client/Hy Farber & Associates, Inc.

299
Advertising
*Artist/***Joe Isom**
Art Director/Joe Isom & Mike Oberlander
Client/West Agro Chemical, Inc.

297
Institutional
*Artist/***David Palladini**
Art Director/Joseph Fazio
Client/Geigy Pharmaceuticals

301
Book
*Artist/***Nicholasa Mohr**
Art Director/Anne Brown
Title/Nilda
Publisher/Harper & Row Publishers, Inc.

300
Editorial
*Artist/***Stan Hunter**
Art Director/Dick Umnitz
Publication/The Literary Guild Magazine

302
Editorial
*Artist/***Paul Giovanopoulos**
Art Director/Neil Shakery
Publication/Saturday Review

303
Film
*Artist/***Len Berzofsky**
Art Director/Len Berzofsky
Production/ABC-TV
Client/Eyewitness News

304
Editorial
*Artist/***David Grove**
Art Director/Neil Shakery
Publication/Saturday Review

305
Book
*Artist/***Charles Mikolaycak**
Art Director/Robert G. Lowe
Title/The Feast Day
Publisher/Little, Brown & Co.

306
Editorial
*Artist/***Mark English**
Art Director/William Cadge
Publication/Redbook

307
Advertising
Artist/**Joe Isom**
Art Director/Joe Isom & Mike Oberlander
Client/West Agro Chemical, Inc.

309
Advertising
Artist/**Joe Isom**
Art Director/Joe Isom & Mike Oberlander
Client/West Agro Chemical, Inc.

308
Book
Artist/**Richard Huebner**
Art Director/Richard Huebner

310
Institutional
*Artist/***Harvey Dinnerstein**
Art Director/Stanley Glaubach
Client/Local 1199, Drug & Hospital Union

311
Editorial
*Artist/***Philip Belbin**
Art Director/Douglas Albion & Edwin Kolsby
Publication/Reader's Digest

312
Book
*Artist/***Bob Pepper**
Art Director/Charles Volpe
Title/LO!
Publisher/Ace Books

313
Institutional
*Artist/***Chet Jeziereski**
Art Director/Chet Jeziereski

314
Advertising
*Artist/***Bernie Karlin**
Art Director/Tony Madia
Agency/Mohr & Co.
Client/Hitemco

315
Institutional
*Artist/***Robert S. Lowery**
Art Director/Robert S. Lowery

316
Advertising
Artist/**Richard Harvey**
Art Director/Neil Terk
Client/Chess/Janus Records

317
Advertising
Artist/**Charles Shields**
Art Director/Tony Lane
Client/Fantasy Records

318
Institutional
Artist/**Lorraine Fox**
Art Director/Lorraine Fox

320
Advertising
*Artist/***Janosch**
Art Director/Victoria Gomez
Client/Lothrop, Lee & Shepard

319
Advertising
*Artist/***Don Ivan Punchatz**
Art Director/A. Neal Siegel
Client/Smith, Kline & French Laboratories

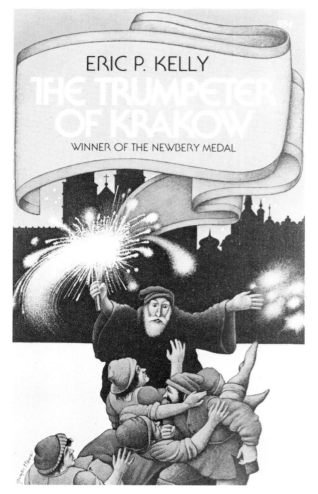

321
Book
*Artist/***Roger Hane**
Art Director/Ava Weiss
Title/The Trumpeter of Krakow
Publisher/The Macmillan Co.

322
Institutional
*Artist/***Margaret Cusack**
Art Director/Margaret Cusack

323
Book
*Artist/***Giulio Maestro**
Art Director/Robert Verrone
Title/The Remarkable Plant in Apartment 4
Publisher/Bradbury Press, Inc.

325
Editorial
*Artist/***Herbert Tauss**
Art Director/Stan Mack
Publication/The New York Times

324
Book
*Artist/***Gene Szafran**
Art Director/Leonard Leone
Title/All The Kings Men
Publisher/Bantam Books

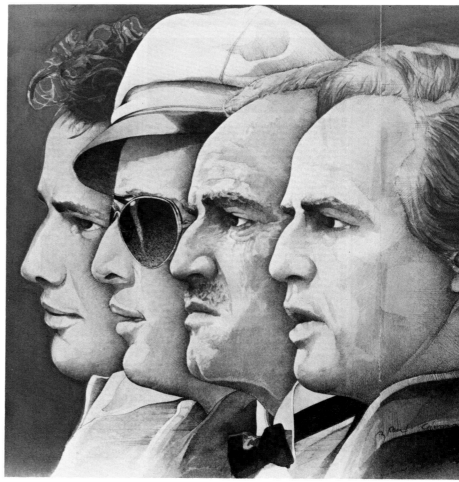

326
Editorial
*Artist/***Paul Giovanopoulos**
Art Director/Walter Bernard
Publication/New York Magazine

327
Book
*Artist/***Charles Moll**
Art Director/Barbara Bertoli
Title/It Never Rains In Los Angeles
Publisher/Avon Books

328
Advertising
*Artist/***Bob Alcorn**
Art Director/Herb Lubalin
Agency/Lubalin, Smith, Carnase
Client/American Film Theatre

329
Book
Artist/**Fred Pfeiffer**
Art Director/Leonard Leone
Title/The Incredible Brazilian
Publisher/Bantam Books, Inc.

330
Institutional
Artist/**Ted CoConis**
Art Director/Jerry Huff
Agency/Milici Advertising
Client/Hawaiian Telephone Co.

331
Book
*Artist/***William Edwards**
Art Director/Leonard Leone
Title/Doctor Brodie's Report
Publisher/Bantam Books, Inc.

332
Books
*Artist/***Herbert Tauss**
Art Director/Herbert Tauss

333
Book
*Artist/***Graham McCallum**
Art Director/Cynthia Basil
Title/The Story of Persephone
Publisher/Morrow Junior Books

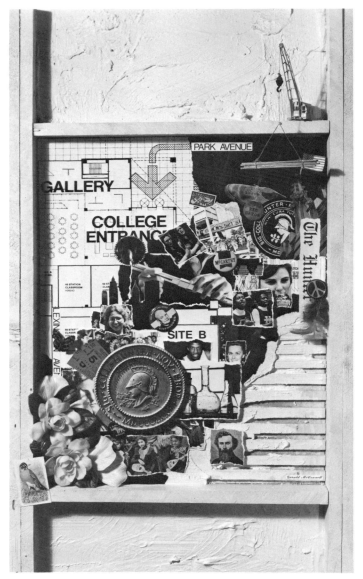

334
Editorial
*Artist/***Gerald McConnell**
Art Director/Pat Molino
Publication/Hunter College Newsletter

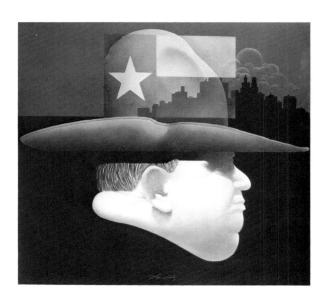

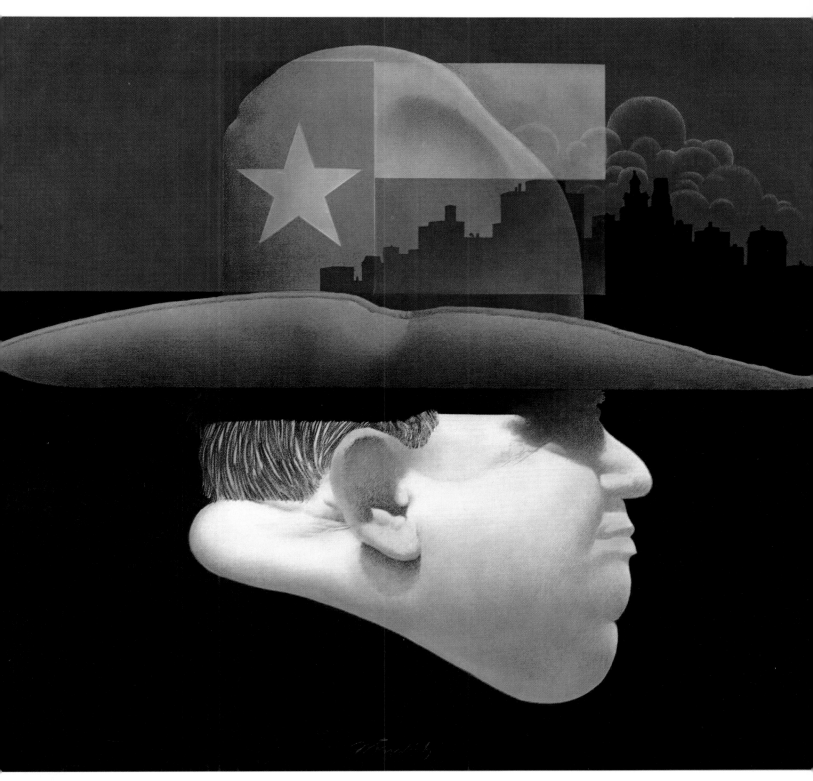

335
Editorial
*Artist/***Mark English**
Art Director/John deCesare
*Publication/*Geigy Pharmaceuticals
Obesity '73 Report
Award of Excellence

337
Institutional
*Artist/**Roy Carruthers***
Art Director/Herb Lubalin
Agency/Lubalin, Smith, Carnase
Client/International Typeface Corp.

336
Book
*Artist/**Roger Kastel***
Art Director/Leonard Leone
Title/I Am Elijah Thrush
Publisher/Bantam Books, Inc.

338
Advertising
*Artist/**Roy Carruthers***
Art Director/Edward Rostock
Agency/Muller, Jordan & Herrick, Inc.
Client/Levolor Lorentzen, Inc.

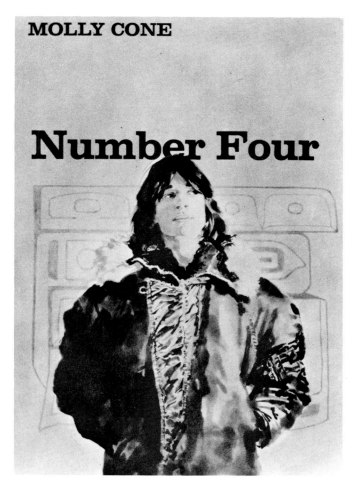

MOLLY CONE

Number Four

339
Book
*Artist/***Ted Lewin**
Art Director/Walter Lorraine
Title/Number Four
Publisher/Houghton Mifflin Co.

340
Editorial
*Artist/***David Passalacqua**
Art Director/Bob McElrath
Publication/Genesis Magazine

341
Institutional
*Artist/***Ron Bradford**
Art Director/Ron Bradford & Al Cout
Agency/Bradford/Cout Design
Client/Franklin Merch

Witches' Brew

**MACBETH
ACT IV SCENE I**

"A recipe" by William Shakespeare,
illustration by Robert J. Lee

301

342
Book
*Artist/***Robert J. Lee**
Art Director/Bill Martin
Title/Witches Brew
Publisher/Holt, Rinehart & Winston, Inc.

343
Institutional
Artist/**Alan E. Cober**
Art Director/Irv Roons
Agency/Irv Roons Associates
Client/Federation of Jewish Philantrophies

344
Advertising
Artist/**Lou Myers**
Art Director/Cullen Rapp
Client/Cullen Rapp, Inc.

345
Advertising
*Artist/***Frank Marciuliano**
Art Director/Nick Giammalvo
Agency/Zakin, Selden, Comerford, Inc.
Client/WVNJ

346
Editorial
*Artist/***Charles Bragg**
Art Director/Arthur Paul
Publication/Playboy Magazine

347
Editorial
*Artist/***David Grove**
Art Director/David Grove
Publication/California Living Magazine

348
Advertising
*Artist/***Kyuzo Tsugami**
Art Director/Kyuzo Tsugami

350
Editorial
*Artist/***Bill Hofmann**
Art Director/Stan Mack
Publication/The New York Times

349
Advertising
*Artist/***Ivan Paslavsky**
Art Director/Ivan Paslavsky

351
Institutional
*Artist/***Gary Overacre**
Art Director/Gary Overacre
Client/Cullen Rapp, Inc.

352
Advertising
Artist/**David Pascal**
Art Director/Hilde Micheli
Client/Immagine

354
Film
Artist/**William S. Shields**
Art Director/Ira Silberlicht
Client/Emergency Medicine

353
Book
Artist/**Howard Rogers**
Art Director/Leonard Leone
Title/The Man Without a Face
Publisher/Bantam Books, Inc.

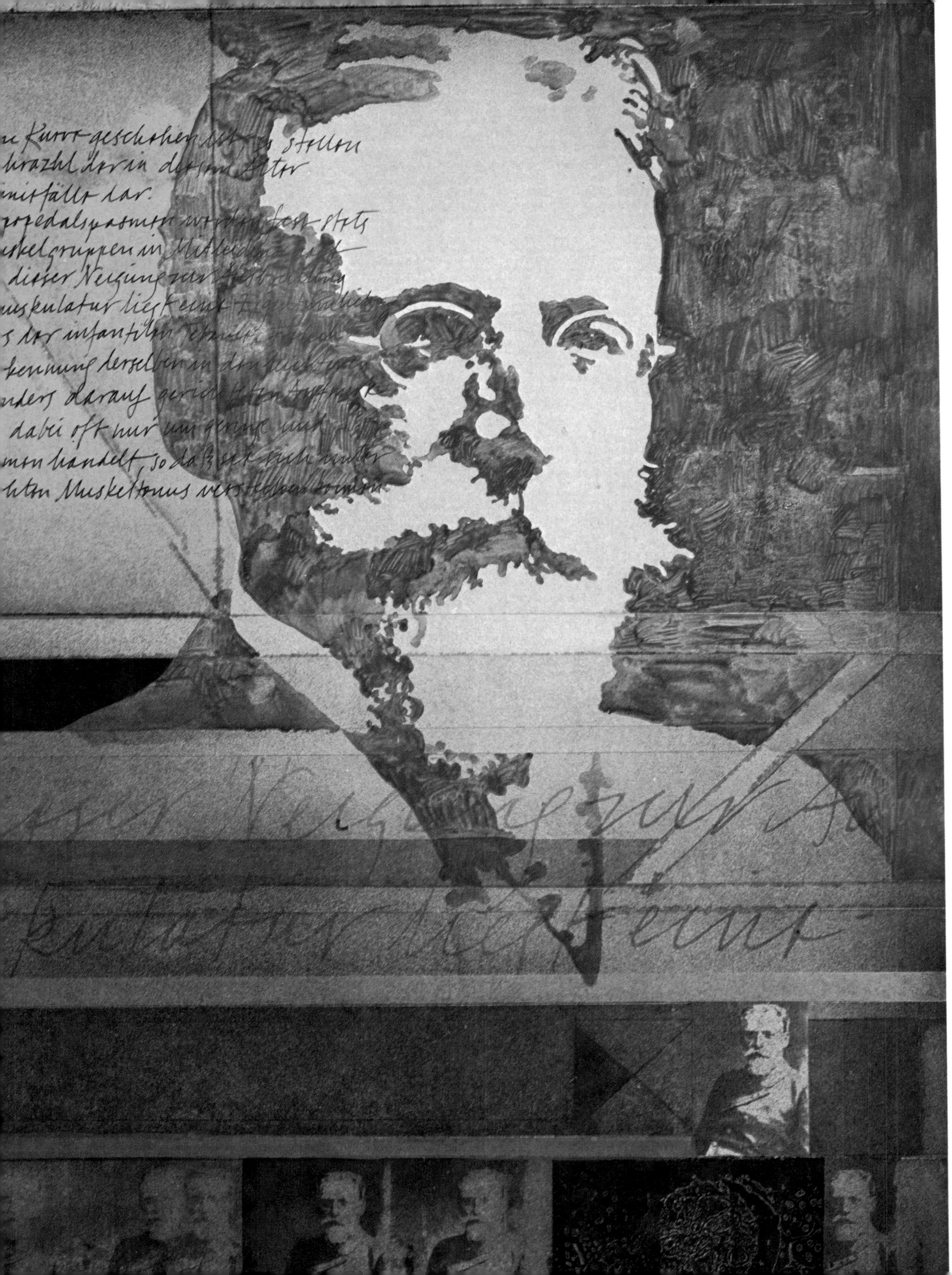

356
Editorial
*Artist/***Vin Giuliani**
Art Director/Harry O. Diamond
Publication/The Lamp

355
Institutional
Artist/Fred Otnes
Art Director/Phil Fiorello
Agency/J. Walter Thompson Co.
Client/Eli Lilly

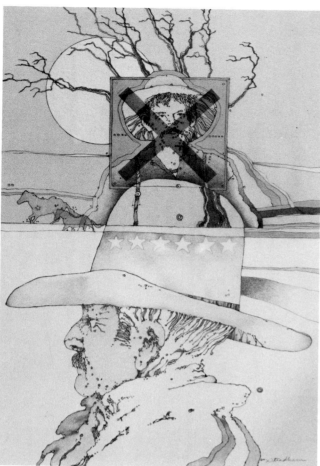

359
Editorial
Artist/**Terry Steadham**
Art Director/*Terry Steadham*
Publication/*Young World Magazine*

361
Editorial
Artist/**Shawn Shea**
Art Director/*Shawn Shea*

360
Book
Artist/**David McCall Johnston**
Art Director/*David McCall Johnston*

363
Institutional
*Artist/**Alan Magee***
Art Director/Alan Magee

364
Book
*Artist/**Bob McGinnis***
Art Director/Barbara Bertoli
Title/Signs & Portents
Publisher/Avon Books

362
Advertising
*Artist/**Richard Hess***
Art Director/John Berg
Client/Columbia Records

365
Institutional
*Artist/***Paul Calle**
Art Director/Roger Core
Agency/Medicus
Client/Schering Laboratories

366
Institutional
*Artist/***Paul Calle**
Art Director/Roger Core
Agency/Medicus
Client/Schering Laboratories

367
Book
Artist/**Paul Calle**
Art Director/Murray J. Miller
Title/Great People of the Bible
Publisher/Reader's Digest Association

368
Book
Artist/**Tom Beecham**
Art Director/Murray J. Miller
Title/Great People of the Bible
Publisher/Reader's Digest Association

369
Institutional
*Artist/***John Berkey**
Art Director/John Berkey

370
Editorial
*Artist/***Frank Bozzo**
Art Director/Skip Sorvino
Publication/Scholastic Magazine

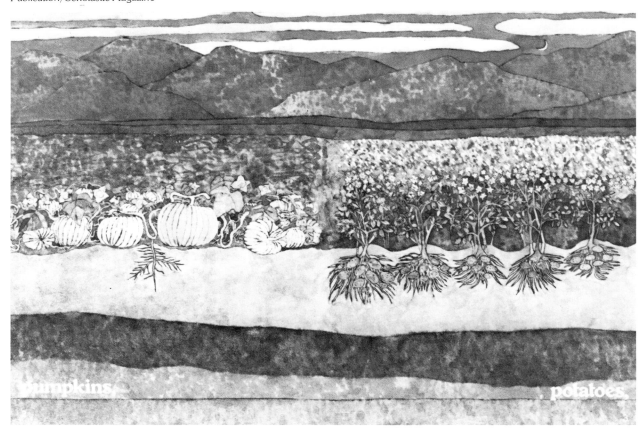

371
Advertising
*Artist/***Nicolas Sidjakov**
Art Director/Maggie Waldron
Agency/Botsford Ketchum, Inc.
Client/Norwegian Canning Industry

372
Editorial
*Artist/***Frank Bozzo**
Art Director/Skip Sorvino
Publication/Scholastic Magazine

Pumpkins, potatoes, celery, and cranberries. For gifts of the earth we give thanks.

373
Book
*Artist/***Tim Hildebrandt & Gregg Hildebrant**
Art Director/Paul L. Taylor
Title/Animal Disguises
Publisher/Bowmar Publishing Corp.

374
Editorial
*Artist/***Alan E. Cober**
Art Director/Richard M. Gangel
Publication/Sports Illustrated

375
Advertising
*Artist/***Alan Magee**
Art Director/Alan Magee
Client/Eric & Martha Nagler

376
Advertising
*Artist/***Don Brautigam**
Art Director/Paula Bisacca
Client/Atlantic Records

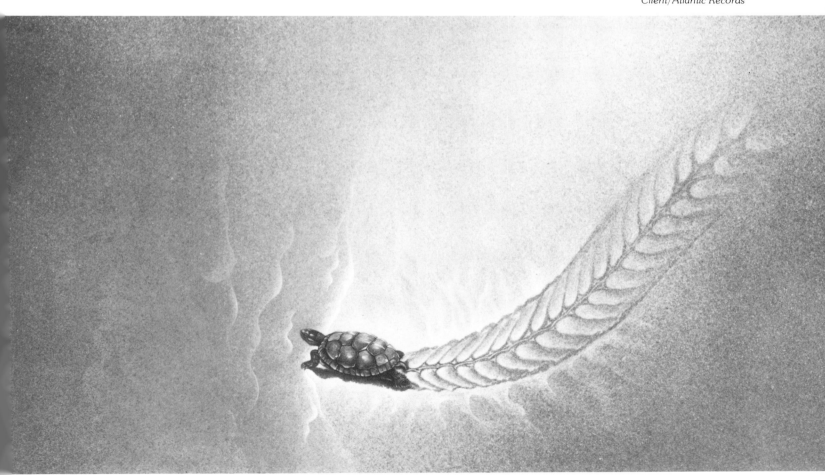

378
Institutional
*Artist/***Fred Thomas**
Art Director/Fred Thomas
Client/Fred & Lilly Parish

377
Advertising
*Artist/***Gene Szafran**
Art Director/Richard Selby
Client/McCall's Magazine

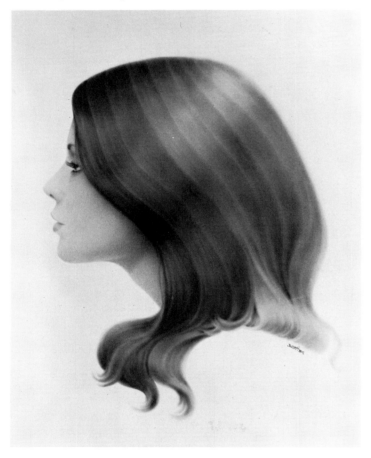

379
Institutional
*Artist/***Alex Gnidziejko**
Art Director/Arthur Beckenstein
Agency/Medcom, Inc.
Client/Wyeth Laboratories

MYSTERIES, MYSTERIES

NO ONE WOULD EVER HAVE SAID AUNT LINY WAS A PROFOUND WOMAN, BUT THANKS TO HER, RUTHIE LEARNED A LITTLE MORE ABOUT WHERE WE COME FROM—AND WHERE WE ARE GOING

My second cousin Woodrow McDermott was born with six toes on one foot and was eight years old before his mother, whom we called Aunt Liny, even noticed it. She said, when it was called to her attention, that by the time you had had 12 children you just weren't up to counting everything—eyes and ears, maybe, but, "Lord in heaven," she said, "who counts toes?"

Well, my mother counted toes, that was who, and—"every other responsible woman since the beginning of time," I heard her tell my father, "and the worst of it is that Liny isn't going to do anything about it."

"I don't know that she can," Daddy said reasonably. "I don't suppose you can just lop off a toe whenever you feel like it."

"Maybe not, but the least Liny could do is investigate," Mother said.

But it wasn't in Aunt Liny's nature to investigate. She took things as they came: good times, bad times; drought or deluge; children—nine living, three dead; Woodrow's six toes; the complete shiftlessness of her husband, Will, who was never / turn to page

BY BARBARA ROBINSON

380
Editorial
Artist/**Alan Magee**
Art Director/Alvin Grossman & Modesto Torre
Publication/McCall's Magazine

381
Advertising
Artist/**Gilbert L. Stone**
Art Director/Les Barany
Client/Dofan Handbag Co., Inc.

382
Institutional
*Artist/***Richard Huebner**
Art Director/Richard Huebner

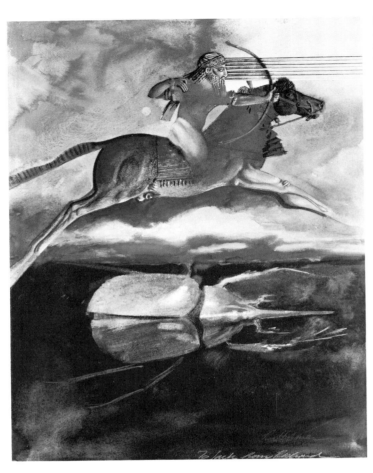

383
Book
*Artist/***James Barkley**
Art Director/Greg Wozney
Publisher/Scholastic Magazines, Inc.

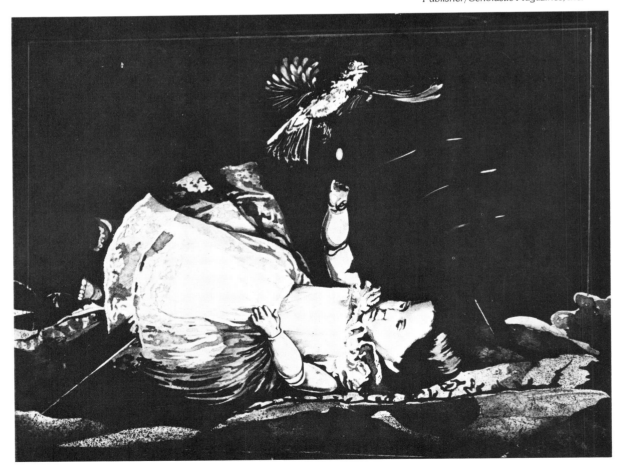

384
Book
*Artist/***Alan E. Cober**
Art Director/Harriet Barton
Title/Eagle
Publisher/Atheneum Publishers

385
Book
*Artist/***Alan E. Cober**
Art Director/Harriet Barton
Title/Horse
Publisher/Atheneum Publishers

386
Institutional
*Artist/***Eugene Tulley**
Art Director/Bill Harkins
Agency/Grant-Jacoby, Inc.

gene tulley

387
Institutional
*Artist/***John Berkey**
Art Director/John Berkey

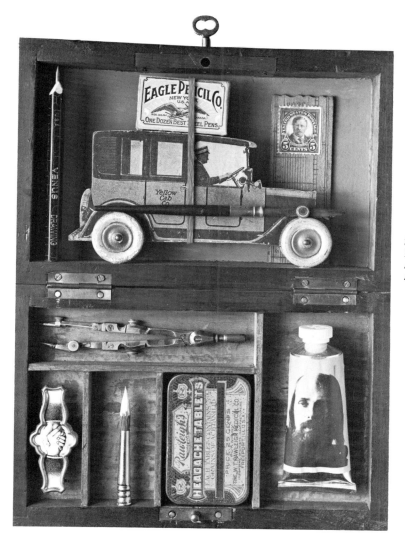

388
Institutional
*Artist/***Wendell Minor**
Art Director/Wendell Minor

389
Advertising
*Artist/***A.K.M. Studios**
Art Director/Acy Lehman
Client/RCA Records

390
Editorial
*Artist/***Murray Tinkelman**
Art Director/J. C. Suares
Publication/The New York Times

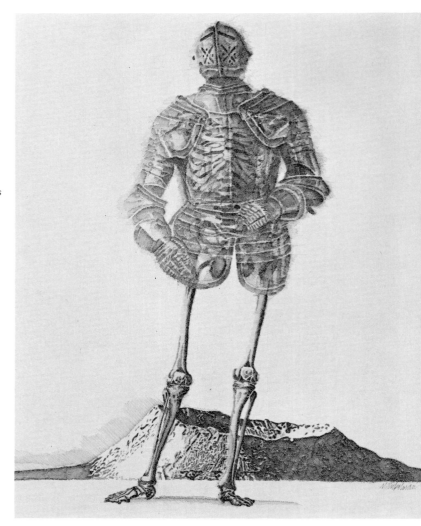

391
Editorial
*Artist/***Murray Tinkelman**
Art Director/R. B. Luden
Publication/Warlock Press

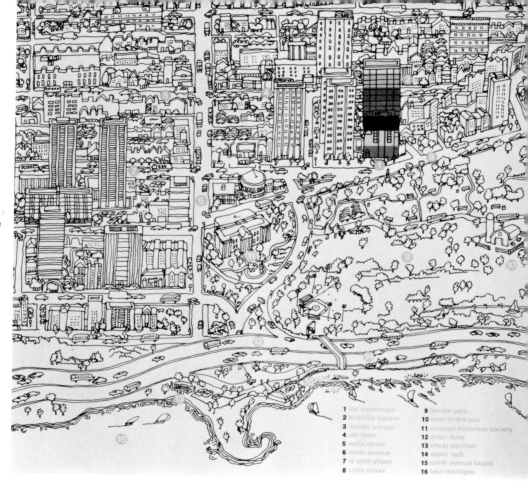

392
Advertising
*Artist/***Terry Rose**
Art Director/Bradford/Cout
Agency/Bradford/Cout Design
Client/M. Myers & Associates

393
Institutional
*Artist/***Richard Kunath**
Art Director/Richard Kunath
Client/Fairleigh Dickinson University

394
Book
*Artist/***Shannon Stirnweis**
Art Director/Shannon Stirnweis

395
Advertising
*Artist/***Nicholas Gaetano**
Art Director/Clark Frankel
Agency/Young & Rubicam, Inc.
Client/Excedrin

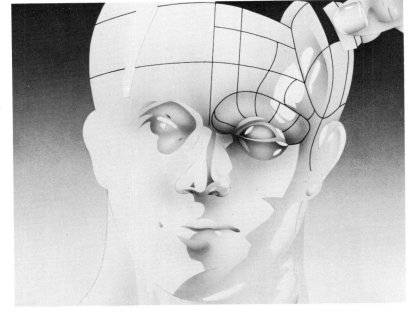

396
Advertising
*Artist/***Burt Groedel**
Art Director/Roy Freemantle
Agency/Gaynor & Ducas, Inc.
Client/Keuffel & Esser Co.

397
Advertising
*Artist/***Romar Beardon**
Art Director/John Berg
Client/Columbia Records

398
Book
*Artist/***Fred Pfeiffer**
Art Director/Leonard Leone
Title/Soul Catcher
Publisher/Bantam Books, Inc.

399
Book
*Artist/***Ralph Pereida**
Art Director/Lester Rossin
Title/Grazing
Publisher/M. Grumbacher Inc.

400
Book
*Artist/***Ken Riley**
Art Director/Leonard Leone
Title/Ishi: Last of His Tribe
Publisher/Bantam Books, Inc.

401
Book
*Artist/***Ted CoConis**
Art Director/Edward Aho
Title/Apollo
Publisher/The Viking Press

403
Institutional
*Artist/***Joseph Ianelli**
Art Director/Richard Wilde
Client/School of Visual Arts

402
Editorial
*Artist/***Ken Dallison**
Art Director/Gene Butera
Publication/Car and Driver Magazine

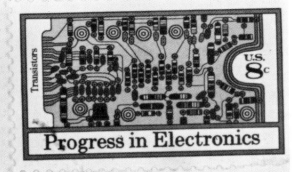

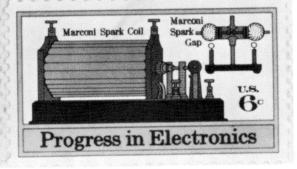

404
Institutional
*Artist/***Naiad & Walter Einsel**
Art Director/Stevan Dohanos
Client/U.S. Postal Service

405
Film
*Artist/***Bob Blansky**
Art Director/Frank Perry
Production/Dolphin Productions
Agency/Fuller & Smith & Ross, Inc.
Client/AMF

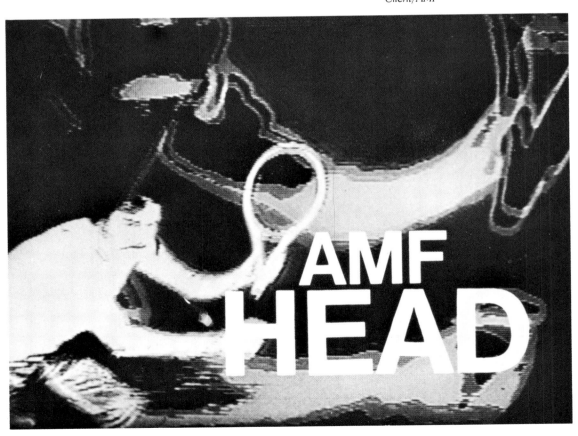

406
Advertising
*Artist/***Bruce Wolfe**
Art Director/Jerry Andeline
Agency/Botsford Ketchum, Inc.
Client/National Potato Board

407
Advertising
*Artist/***Wilson McLean**
Art Director/Sue Forman
Agency/Gilbert, Felix, Sharf, Inc.
Client/Nikon, Inc.

408
Editorial
*Artist/***Stan Hunter**
Art Director/Dick Umnitz
Publication/The Literary Guild Magazine

409
Advertising
*Artist/***David A. Leffel**
Art Director/Bob Ciano
Client/CTI Records

410
Book
*Artist/***Patric Foursh́e**
Art Director/Patric Foursh́e

411
Advertising
*Artist/***Robert Peak**
Art Director/Joe Fiorino
Client/Trans World Airlines

412
Book
*Artist/***Robert Giusti**
Art Director/Jack Ribik
Title/American in Legend
Publisher/Random House, Inc.

413
Advertising
*Artist/***Robert Peak**
Art Director/Joe Fiorino
Client/Trans World Airlines

414
Editorial
Artist/**Richard Ely**
Art Director/James Craig
Publication/American Artist

415
Advertising
*Artist/***George S. Gaadt**
Art Director/Richard Blakemore & Bob Carr
Agency/Pitt Studios
Client/Hammermill Paper Co.

416
Editorial
*Artist/***Gerrie Blake**
Art Director/Tom Gould
Publication/Psychology Today

417
Institutional
*Artist/***David Palladini**
Art Director/David Palladini

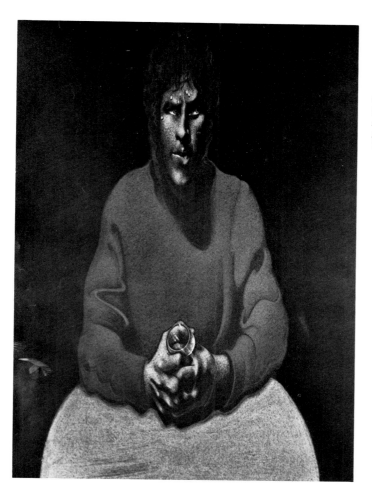

418
Editorial
*Artist/***Gilbert L. Stone**
Art Director/Arthur Paul
Publication/Playboy Magazine

420
Advertising
*Artist/***Gilbert L. Stone**
Art Director/Herb Lubalin
Agency/Lubalin, Smith, Carnase
Client/American Film Theatre

419
Advertising
*Artist/***William Falkenburg**
Art Director/William Falkenburg
Agency/Falkenburg Graphic Illustration
Client/Grubneklaf Graphic Art Gallery

MOVING

It was all very well for Dan- he had a brand-new challenge. And the children didn't seem to mind at all. Why was she the only one who felt uprooted, as if she never again would be at home?
BY MEG CAMPBELL

"Higher."
"What?"
Lindsay shut her teeth in rage. The tiny muscle under her left eyelid began to jump irregularly. "I said lift it higher."

It was ten o'clock on a June morning and already hot as a sauna. They were loading plants into the rented trailer, plants and spray cans and paint and anything else the movers had been too critical to hurl into their big yellow van.

"Okay," said Dan nastily, ignoring the don't-tread-on-me in her voice.

It had been tacitly established early in their marriage that only one got to indulge in bad temper at a time. The other was supposed to be conciliatory until things leveled off. But it had been her turn so long that Dan was getting edgy.

The tall dracaena plant, too lofty to stand upright, had to be propped at a precarious 45-degree angle against one wall of the trailer. Dan yanked at it. Some dirt fell onto the floor of the trailer. "There is a three-dollar fine for returning this trailer in a soiled condition," Lindsay read from a notice pasted on the floor. Some responsible person will have to remember to sweep out the back before we turn it in. I wonder who that worthy soul will be. She was beginning to enjoy this, wallowing in self-pity / turn to page

422
Editorial
Artist/**Bart Forbes**
Art Director/Alvin Grossman & Modesto Torre
Publication/McCall's Magazine

421
Book
Artist/**Fred Otnes**
Art Director/Dhyana Hollingsworth
Title/Discovering American History
Publisher/Holt, Rinehart & Winston, Inc.

423
Editorial
Artist/**Ken Dallison**
Art Director/Robert Hallock
Publication/Lithopinion

Extinct is forever.

427
Book
*Artist/***Leo & Diane Dillon**
Art Director/Atha Tehon
Title/Behind the Back of the Mountain
Publisher/The Dial Press

428
Book
*Artist/***Ray Cruz**
Art Director/Phil Slater
Title/Jungle Sounds
Publisher/Scholastic Books

429
Film
*Artist/***Franklin McMahon**
Art Director/Franklin McMahon
Production/Rocinante Sight & Sound
Client/WBBM-TV, U.S. Steel—CBS

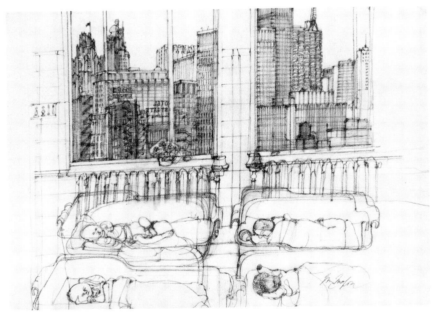

430
Institutional
*Artist/***Franklin McMahon**
Art Director/Robert Lipman & Ronald Olmsted
Client/Northwestern Memorial Hospital

431
Institutional
*Artist/***Franklin McMahon**
Art Director/Robert Burns
Client/U.S. Catholic

432
Editorial
Artist/**Bernard Fuchs**
Art Director/*Robert Hallock*
Publication/*Lithopinion*

433
Editorial
Artist/**Bernard Fuchs**
Art Director/*Robert Hallock*
Publication/*Lithopinion*

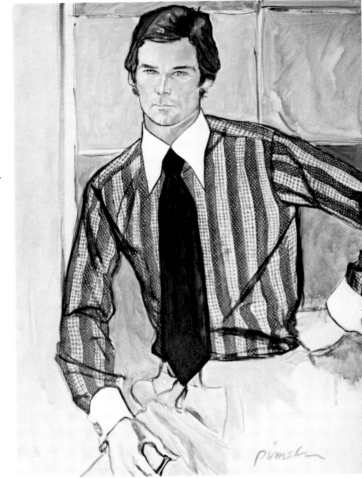

434
Advertising
*Artist/***Alvin J. Pimsler**
Art Director/Alvin J. Pimsler

435
Book
*Artist/***Vincent Petragnani**
Art Director/Vincent Petragnani

436
Advertising
*Artist/***Wilson McLean**
Art Director/Les Friedman
Agency/Edward M. Meyers Associates, Inc.
Client/Phoenix Clothes

437
Editorial
*Artist/***Wilson McLean**
Art Director/Arthur Paul
Publication/Playboy Magazine

439
Advertising
*Artist/***George R. Macalla**
Art Director/Dick Loader
Client/Pitt Studios

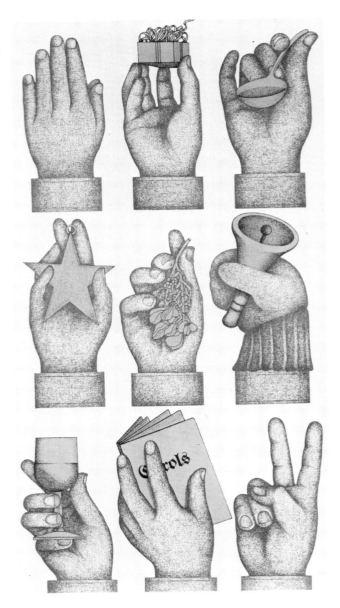

438
Institutional
*Artist/***Esther Harris**
Art Director/Esther Harris

440
*Artist/***Frank Bozzo**
Art Director/Acy Lehman & Joe Stelmach
Client/RCA Records

441
Advertising
*Artist/***Wendell Minor**
Art Director/Kent Salisbury
Agency/Salisbury Associates
Client/Cue Magazine

442
Advertising
*Artist/***Bruce Wolfe**
Art Director/Bruce Wolfe

443
Advertising
*Artist/***Philip Wende**
Art Director/Richard Henderson
Agency/Cole, Henderson, Drake, Inc.
Client/Aviation Insurance

444
Institutional
*Artist/***Shannon Stirnweis**
Art Director/Lt. Col. Tom Holbert
Client/United States Air Force

445
Institutional
*Artist/***Doris Rodewig**
Art Director/Doris Rodewig
Client/United States Air Force

446
Institutional
*Artist/***Robert Boston**
Art Director/Robert Boston

447
Editorial
*Artist/**Barron Storey***
Art Director/Bud Loader
Publication/Flying Magazine

448
Editorial
*Artist/**Barron Storey***
Art Director/Bud Loader
Publication/Flying Magazine

449
Institutional
*Artist/***Daniel Schwartz**
Art Director/Ronald Campbell

450
Institutional
*Artist/***Daniel Schwartz**
Art Director/Ronald Campbell

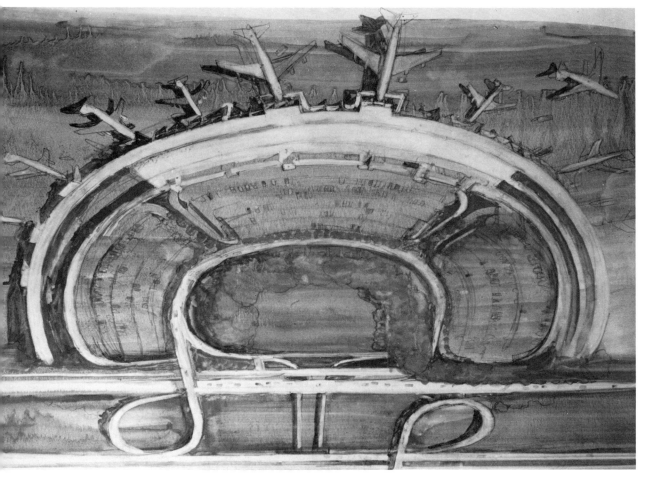

451
Institutional
*Artist/***Robert Byrd**
Art Director/Jack Byrne & Lou Ford
Agency/Ford, Byrne & Brennan
Client/Insurance Company of North America

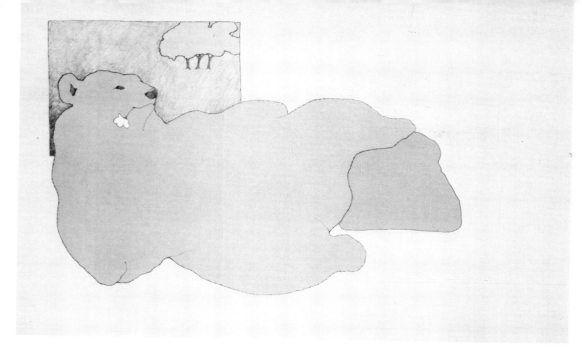

452
Book
*Artist/***Nancy Tafuri**
Art Director/Nancy Tafuri

453
Book
*Artist/***Nancy Tafuri**
Art Director/Nancy Tafuri

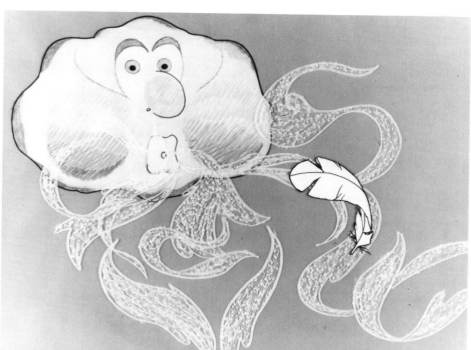

454
Film
*Artist/***Art Babbitt**
Art Director/Art Babbitt
Production/Hanna-Barbera Productions
Client/Marschalk Advertising, Inc.

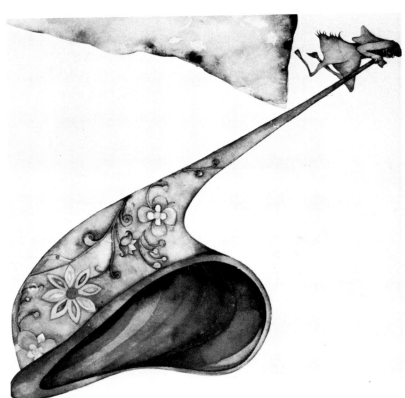

455
Book
*Artist/***Patric Fourshé**
Art Director/Patric Fourshé

456
Advertising
*Artist/***Carole Kowalchuk**
Art Director/Carole Kowalchuk

457
Institutional
*Artist/***Philip Fazio**
Art Director/Philip Fazio

PAIN: A
PASSION
OF THE
SOUL

ARISTOTLE

458
Advertising
*Artist/***Mark English**
Art Director/Frank Wagner
Agency/Sudler & Hennessey, Inc.
Client/Pfizer Laboratories

459
Advertising
*Artist/***John Berkey**
Art Director/Carl Herman
Client/Science Fiction Book Club

460
Book
*Artist/***John Berkey**
Art Director/Barbara Bertoli
Title/20-20 Vision
Publisher/Avon Books

461
Institutional
*Artist/***Robert Boston**
Art Director/Robert Boston

462
Advertising
*Artist/***John Berkey**
Art Director/Jerry Egers
Agency/J. Walter Thompson Co.

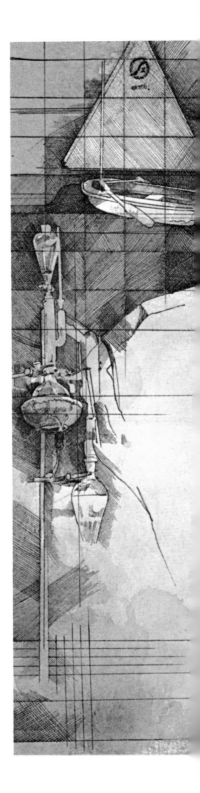

463
Editorial
*Artist/***Vin Giuliani**
Art Director/Harry O. Diamond
Publication/The Lamp

464
Advertising
*Artist/***Christine Duke**
Art Director/Marge Ware
Agency/Campbell-Ewald Co., Inc.
Client/Libby-Owens-Ford Co.

465
Editorial
*Artist/***Robert A. Weaver**
Art Director/Henry Wolf
Publication/Sesame St. Magazine

466
Editorial
*Artist/***Milton Glaser**
Art Director/Henry Wolf
Publication/Sesame Street Magazine

467
Editorial
*Artist/***Michael Gross**
Art Director/John Newcomb
Publication/Golf Digest

468
Editorial
*Artist/***Milton Glaser**
Art Director/Henry Wolf
Publication/Sesame Street Magazine

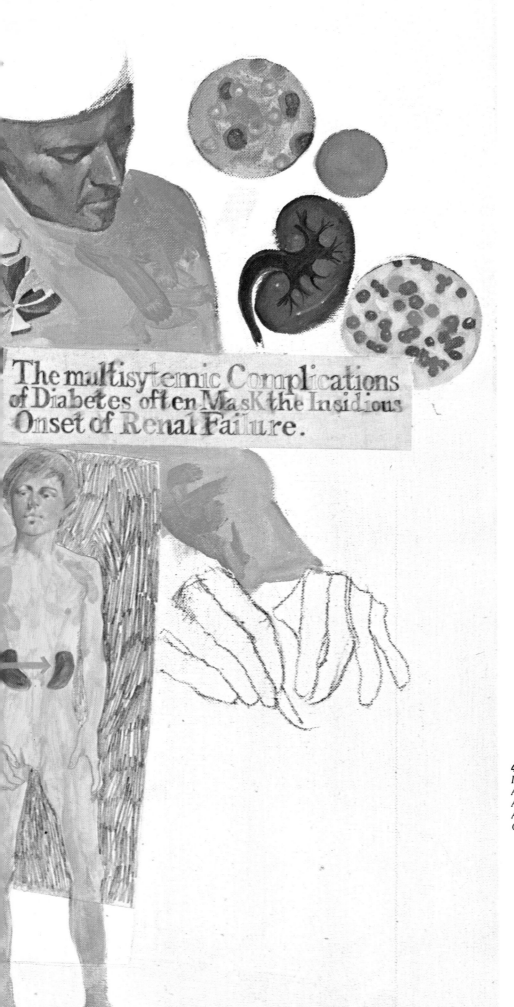

The multisytemic Complications of Diabetes often Mask the Insidious Onset of Renal Failure.

469
Institutional
*Artist/***Robert Baxter**
Art Director/Gary Olivo
Agency/Medcom, Inc.
Client/Warner/Chilcott

470
Book
*Artist/***Alice & Martin Provensen**
Art Director/Grace Clark
Title/My Little Hen
Publisher/Random House, Inc.

471
Book
*Artist/***Midge Quenell**
Art Director/Paul L. Taylor
Title/Going Places
Publisher/Bowmar Publishing Corp.

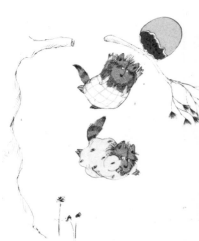

472
Book
*Artist/***Rosemary Wells**
Art Director/Atha Tehon
Title/Benjamin and Tulip
Publisher/The Dial Press

473
Book
*Artist/****Gordon Laite***
Art Director/Paul L. Taylor
Title/Now That Days Are Colder
Publisher/Bowmar Publishing Corp.

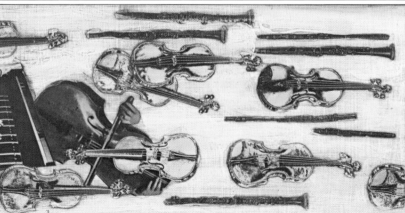

474
Advertising
*Artist/***Cliff Condak**
Art Director/John Berg
Client/Columbia Records

475
Book
Artist/**James Barkley**
Art Director/Sallie Baldwin
Title/The Minstrel Knight
Publisher/Thomas Y. Crowell Co.

476
Editorial
*Artist/***Roger Hane**
Art Director/Alvin Grossman
Publication/McCall's Magazine

**PLANTING
A
PORTABLE
TREE**

477
Editorial
*Artist/***Roger Hane**
Art Director/Alvin Grossman
Publication/McCall's Magazine

478
Institutional
*Artist/***Raymond Ameijide**
Art Director/Dave Perkins
Agency/Aves Advertising
Client/Center for Environmental Study

479
Advertising
*Artist/***Hugo Bossard**
Art Director/Frank A. Lipari
Client/Gazette Canadian Printing

An Exhibit of 1972 Children's Books of Outstanding Graphic Merit

Sponsored by The Children's Book Council in cooperation with
Drexel University and The Free Library of Philadelphia

Date   March 19 - April 7, 1973
        Open daily 9:00 AM - 9:00 PM
Place   Nesbitt Hall, Drexel University
        33rd & Market Streets
        Philadelphia, Pennsylvania
Judges Roger Duvoisin
        Edward Gorey
        Ursula Nordstrom
        Ava Weiss

CHILDREN'S BOOK SHOWCASE

480
Advertising
*Artist/***Jose & Ariane Aruego**
Art Director/Christine Stawicki
Client/The Children's Book Council

481
Film
*Artist/***Phil Smith**
Art Director/Howard Imhoff
Agency/Doremus & Co.
Client/The Dime Savings Bank

Adventures with a Three-Spined Stickleback
A Creative Expression Book

482
Book
*Artist/***Seymour Chwast**
*Art Director/***Skip Sorvino & Phil Slater**
*Title/Adventures with a
Three Spined Stickleback*
Publisher/Scholastic Books

483
Book
*Artist/***Camille Norman**
Art Director/Camille Norman

484
Book
*Artist/***Steven R. Kidd**
Art Director/Steven R. Kidd

So they took it away,
and were married next de
By the turkey who lives on the hill.

485A, B, C
Film
*Artist/***Lou Sayer Schwartz**
Art Director/Richard Schneider & Sal Lazzarotti
Client/Guideposts Magazine

487
Advertising
*Artist/***Bart Forbes**
Art Director/Bart Forbes

486
Book
*Artist/***Roger Kastel**
Art Director/Leonard Leone
Title/It's Not the End of the World
Publisher/Bantam Books, Inc.

488
Editorial
*Artist/***Carol Wald**
Art Director/Robert Clive
Publication/Life Magazine

489
Advertising
*Artist/***Raymond Kursar**
Art Director/Allen P. Golden
Client/American Artists Group

490
Editorial
*Artist/***Robert Vickrey**
Art Director/Alvin Grossman & Modesto Torre
Publication/McCall's Magazine

491
Editorial
Artist/**Howard Koslow**
Art Director/Howard Koslow

492
Institutional
Artist/**Charles Shaw**
Art Director/Charles Shaw
Client/General Land Office, Austin, Texas

493
Advertising
*Artist/***George S. Gaadt**
Art Director/Ron Chory
Agency/Fahlgren & Associates, Inc.
Client/McDonough Incentive Division

494
Institutional
*Artist/***Charles Shaw**
Art Director/Charles Shaw
Client/General Land Office, Austin, Texas

495
Editorial
Artist/**Alex Ebel**
Art Director/Arthur Paul
Publication/Playboy Magazine

496
Film
Artist/**Phil Smith**
Art Director/Howard Imhoff
Agency/Doremus & Co.
Client/The Dime Savings Bank

497
Advertising
Artist/**Jerry Pinkney**
Art Director/Richard Trask
Agency/Don Wise & Co.
Client/Scovill Manufacturing

498
Film
Artist/**Phil Smith**
Art Director/Howard Imhoff
Agency/Doremus & Co.
Client/The Dime Savings Bank

499
Book
Artist/**Leigh Grant**
Art Director/Leigh Grant

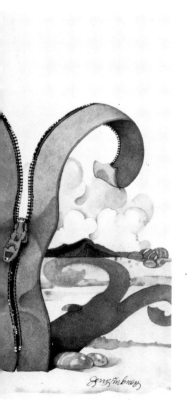

500
Advertising
*Artist/***Guy Billout**
Art Director/Louis Portuesi
Client/Reader's Digest

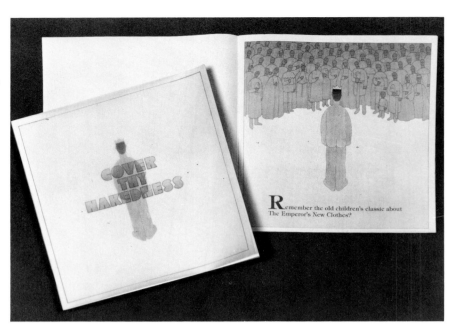

501
Advertising
*Artist/***Guy Billout**
Art Director/Louis Portuesi
Client/Reader's Digest

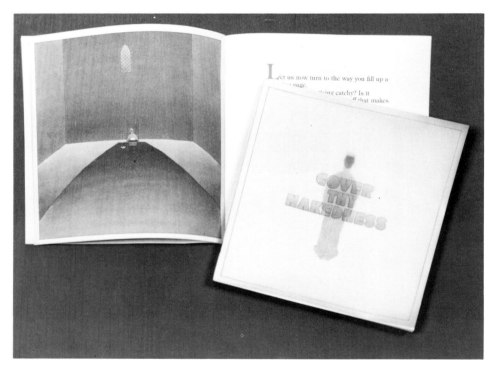

502
Book
*Artist/***Robert E. Weaver**
Art Director/Robert E. Weaver

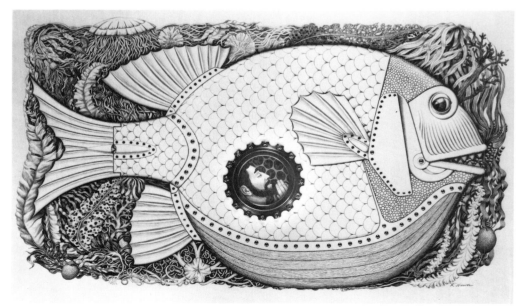

503
Editorial
*Artist/***Arthur Singer**
Art Director/Charles O. Hyman
Publication/National Geographic

504
Advertising
*Artist/***Beverly Wende**
Art Director/Dan Scarlotto
Agency/Cargill, Wilson & Acree, Inc.
Client/Punta Gorda Isles

505
Institutional
*Artist/**Charles Varner***
Art Director/Harrell Moten
Client/Texas Christian University

506
Institutional
*Artist/**Richard Hess***
Art Director/Leslie A. Segal
Agency/Corporate Annual Reports
Client/Scovill Manufacturing Co.

507
Advertising
*Artist/***Don Almquist**
Art Director/Arthur Ludwig
Agency/Dick Jones Designs
Client/Schering Corp., U.S.A.

508
Advertising
*Artist/***Don R. Tate**
Art Director/Stan Sczepanski
Agency/Flair Merchandising, Inc.
Client/International Harvester Co.

509
Editorial
*Artist/***Bernard Fuchs**
Art Director/Richard M. Gangel
Publication/Sports Illustrated

510
Editorial
*Artist/***Alan Magee**
Art Director/Alvin Grossman & Modesto Torre
Publication/McCall's Magazine

LAST TRAIN TO ELM GROVE

All my life I'd heard that you can't go home again. But Grandpa did—and took me with him

One old man had come all the way from Detroit—over 200 miles—just to make this last run from Scioto Station to Elm Grove; traveled 200 miles to ride 30 miles one way, 30 miles the other. He didn't tell us that, didn't advertise himself in any way; but the conductor, who looked exactly as old, as shabby and as used up as the one-car train itself, stopped short when he saw this man and nearly dropped his ticket punch.

"My God!" the conductor said. "Billy Wilson!"

His profanity shocked me a little, although I was with Grandpa, whose language was so consistently yeasty, so well larded with references to the world, the Lord, the flesh and the devil that I should have been immune to such shock.

Then the conductor went from person to person, telling us all that that was Billy Wilson, who used to ride the Elm Grove spur years ago and had returned / *turn to page 128*

BY BARBARA ROBINSON

511
Institutional
*Artist/***Bruce Macdonald**
Art Director/Bruce Macdonald

512
Editorial
*Artist/***Donald Moss**
Art Director/Richard M. Gangel
Publication/Sports Illustrated

513
Editorial
*Artist/***Donald Moss**
Art Director/Richard M. Gangel
Publication/Sports Illustrated

514
Institutional
*Artist/***Lionel Kalish**
Art Director/Bob Englund
Agency/Batten, Barton, Durstine & Osborn, Inc.
Client/3M Company

515
Book
*Artist/***Seymour Chwast**
Art Director/Eleanor Ehrhardt
Title/This is the House that Jack Built
Publisher/Random House, Inc.

This is the cock that crowed in the morn,
That waked the priest all shaven and shorn,
That married the man all tattered and torn,
That kissed the maiden all forlorn,
That milked the cow with the crumpled horn,
That tossed the dog,
That worried the cat,
That killed the rat,
That ate the malt
That lay in the house that Jack built.

Advertisements

Jane Sneyd, Advertising Director

ADVERTISERS

ILLUSTRATORS 16

design
illustration
production

Kirchoff / Wohlberg

331 East 50 Street, New York, New York 10022 212-753-5146
589 Boston Post Road, Madison, Connecticut 06443 203-245-7308

Representing: Angela Adams William Amos Robert Binks Paul Blakey Beatrice Darwin Arlene Dubanevich Alex Ebel Lois
Ehlert Janice Forberg Rosalind Fry Tom Funk Nahid Haghighat Erik Hansen Morgan Harris Hilary Hayton Phyllis Herfield
Margaret Hill Rosekrans Hoffman Gerry Hoover Fred Irvin Harvey Kidder Gordon Laite Don Leake Dora Leder Ron LeHew
Richard Loehle Don Madden Stefan Martin Erica Merkling Jane Nelson Carol Nicklaus Nickzad Nodjoumi Stephen Osborn
Judy Pelikan Susan Perl Jan Pyk Joseph Smith Douglas Snow Arvis Stewart Karl Stuecklen Phero Thomas John Wallner

THOSE WONDERFUL FOLKS AT HRW

who brought you
Einstein's Theory of Relativity
Fear of Flying
Modern Biology
Bury My Heart at Wounded Knee
Collected Works of Robert Frost
Mary Roberts Rinehart
Snoopy
(to name only a few)

HAVE MORE WONDERS IN STORE FOR YOU

Holt, Rinehart and Winston artists, writers, editors...
are helping millions gain new insights into the
changing world around them through all kinds of books.

HOLT, RINEHART AND WINSTON, PUBLISHERS,
a division of CBS, INC., 383 Madison Avenue, New York, N.Y. 10017 Atlanta/Chicago/Dallas/San Francisco

1 TRINA HYMAN 2 JAMES ARNOSKY 3 LOWELL HESS
4 EVA CELLINI 5 MIKE EAGLE 6 PAMELA CARROLL
7 HELENE WILEY 8 SUZANNE VALLA 9 DENNY HAMPSON
10 DONNA DIAMOND
11 ORIN KINCADE 12 TONIA HAMPSON 13 WALTER CARROLL
14 JOSEPH CELLINI 15 RANDY JONES 16 LORNA TOMEI

DICK MORRILL INC
210 E 47TH ST
NEW YORK 10017
421 5833
CONTACT DICK MORRILL
OR BARBARA HELD

Artists International

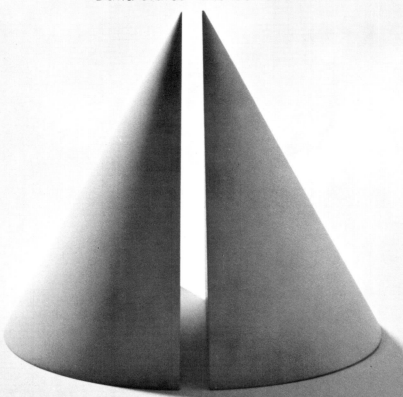

John Alcorn	John Holmes
Gino d'Achille	Roberto Innocenti
Sal Catalano	Norman MacDonald
Tony Chen	Alan Manham
Heather Cooper	Betty Maxey
Jennifer Eachus	Anne Meisel
Brian Froud	Jennifer Perrott
David Graves	Michael Turner

Representing exceptional illustrators from the U.S.A. and around the world in the fields of paperbacks, childrens books, reference books, schoolbooks, editorial and advertising.

We also represent <u>TV Cartoons</u> (London), for your production needs in animated television commercials and feature films.

In the USA: Artists International, 67 East 80th Street, New York 10021. Michael G. Brodie (212) 249 5760. Telex: 424638ARTI and 66447ARTI. Cables: Sunsetone
In the UK: Artist Partners Ltd, 14 Ham Yard, London WIV8DE 01-734 7991. Telex: 24449LEROI.

DON MOSS
APPEARS AND
DISAPPEARS
ON THE PAGES OF
SPORTS ILLUSTRATED

WALTER RANE

GEORGE JONES

DON SILVERSTEIN

BEN WOHLBERG

WALTER RANE

BOB BERRAN

HOWARD TERPNING

BIRNEY LETTICK

HECTOR GARRIDO

ROBERT HEINDEL

DON STIVERS

VAN KAUFMAN

MIKE SMOLLIN

FRANK WAGNER

ULDIS KLAVINS

BILL MAUGHAN

ROBERT HEINDEL

JIM CAMPBELL

the "empty nest syndrome"

MARILYN CONOVER

MIKE SMOLLIN

HOWARD ROGERS

GORDON JOHNSON

BILL MAUGHAN

VAN KAUFMAN

DAVID McCALL JOHNSTON

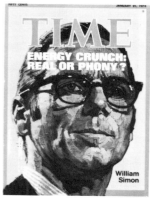

TYPE O
Round nibs (14) for freehand lettering and sketching. (Also 13 sizes of TYPE R tubular nibs for use with lettering guides.)

0.2 0.3 0.4 0.5 0.6 0.7 0.8 1.0 1.25 1.6 2.0 2.5 3.2 5.0

TYPE N
Right-hand slant nibs for oblique lines.

0.8 1.25 2.0 2.5 3.2 4.0

TYPE Z
Left-hand slant nibs for oblique lines.

0.8 1.25 2.0 3.2

Artwork created by utilizing all 60 nibs of the Graphos system, designated above in millimeters.

and lettering work with drawing ink.

Graphos assortments—packed in attractive cases—are available in "College", "Standard" (shown) and "Master" sets.

KOH-I-NOOR

Exclusive *Pelikan* Representative

McDERMOTT / BOB McGINNIS / ED McLAUGHLIN / ALAN MAGEE / MARA McAFEE / PAUL BACON / JO
SCHWALB / DICK KENNERSON / ELAINE DUILLO / DEAN ELLIS / TOM MILLER / CHARLIE MOLL / MIKE STR
POPP / DICK POWERS / GENE SZAFRAN / HERB TAUSS / GEORGE SOTTUNG / HAL SEIGEL / WALTER ST
McCANCE / SAUL MANDEL / LOU MARCHETTI / RITA FLODEN LEYDON / JERRY PODWIL / WHITNEY DARR
MARCUS / ELLIOT SCHNEIDER / NORMAN GREEN / JOAN GREENFIELD / GEORGE GROSS / BLAKE HAMPT
LEHR / BIRNEY LETTICK / HARRY BENNETT / PETER CARAS / JOHN CHILLY / TED COCONIS / GIL COHEN
O ACCONERO / GEORGE ALVARO / BILL WEIKH / LESTER KRAUSS / MURIEL NASSER / JIM AVATI / ANN
ASON / BARNEY THOMPSON / JACK THURSTON / BILL WENZEL / STAN BORACK / JACK BRESLOW / DA
LIEBLEIN / OSCAR LIEBMAN / JOE LOMBARDERO / JOHN BERKEY / CHARLIE MOLL / BOB CUEVAS / ANN
PREZIO / DON PUNCHATZ / DORIS RODEWIG / HOWARD ROGERS / DON MOSS / BIL KEANE / HANK
OOKS / CHET JEZIERSKI / BILL JOHNSON / STUART KAUFMAN / NORMAN ADAMS / HECTOR GARRIDO
AGUIRE / FRANK FRAZETTA / STAN GALLI / CHARLIE GEHM / ALLAN MARDON / RONNIE LESSER / JACK D
KNIGHT / DICK KOHFIELD / ROLF ERIKSON / CARL HANTMAN / JOHNNY HART / HARRY KANE / MORT K
ASON / BARNEY THOMPSON / JACK THURSTON / BILL WENZEL / STAN BORACK / JACK BRESLOW / DAN
O ACCONERO / GEORGE ALVARO / BILL WEIKH / LESTER KRAUSS / MURIEL NASSER / JIM AVATI / ANN
LIEBLEIN / OSCAR LIEBMAN / JOE LOMBARDERO / IRVING BERNSTEIN / JOHN MELO / TOM MILLER / CHAR
KRESEK / MORT KUNSTLER / PAUL LEHR / BIRNEY LETTICK / CARL HANTMAN / JOHNNY HART / JOHN Mc
AN GREEN / JOAN GREENFIELD / GEORGE GROSS / BLAKE HAMPTON / SAUL MANDEL / LOU MARCHETT
OOKS / CHET JEZIERSKI / BILL JOHNSON / STUART KAUFMAN / BIL KEANE / HANK KETCHAM / STAN KLI
E MOLL / BARNEY THOMPSON / JACK THURSTON / BILL WENZEL / BILL TEASON / HARRY BENNETT / HE
ORNELL / BOB CUEVAS / ANN DALTON / ALLAN MARDON / ELAINE DUILLO / JOHN BERKEY / ELLIOT SCH
N McDERMOTT / BOB McGINNIS / ED McLAUGHLIN / ALAN MAGEE / MARA McAFEE / PAUL BACON / JO
LODEN LEYDON / PETER CARAS / JOHN CHILLY / TED COCONIS / GIL COHEN / LEW McCANCE / GENE
KNIGHT / DICK KOHFIELD / JERRY PODWIL / WALTER POPP / DICK POWERS / BOB McGINNIS / ED McLAU
TOR GARRIDO / CHARLIE GEH KSON / LESTER KRAUSS / WALTER
LEHR / BIRNEY LETTICK / HARRY Y / TED COCONIS / GIL COHEN /
RY MARCUS / ELLIOT SCHNEID LD / GEORGE GROSS / BLAKE HAM
McCANCE / SAUL MANDEL / LC / JERRY PODWIL / WHITNEY DARR
LTER POPP / DICK POWERS / C E SOTTUNG / HAL SEIGEL / WALTER
LIE MOLL / BARNEY THOMPSON / JACK THURSTON / BILL WENZEL / BILL TEASON / HARRY BENNETT / H
E HOOKS / CHET JEZIERSKI / BILL JOHNSON / STUART KAUFMAN / BIL KEANE / HANK KETCHAM / STAN K
MAN GREEN / JOAN GREENFIELD / GEORGE GROSS / BLAKE HAMPTON / SAUL MANDEL / LOU MARCHE
KRESEK / MORT KUNSTLER / PAUL LEHR / BIRNEY LETTICK / CARL HANTMAN / JOHNNY HART / JOHN Mc
I LIEBLEIN / OSCAR LIEBMAN / JOE LOMBARDERO / IRVING BERNSTEIN / JOHN MELO / TOM MILLER / CH
Y KNIGHT / DICK KOHFIELD / JERRY PODWIL / WALTER POPP / DICK POWERS / BOB McGINNIS / ED McLA
SCHULZ / SUSAN SCHWALB / VICTOR PREZIO / DON MOSS / TONY FERRARA / JACK DAVIS / JEFF JONES
OR GARRIDO / CHARLIE GEHM / JIM AVATI / PAUL BACON / ROLF ERIKSON / LESTER KRAUSS / WALTER ST
ASON / BARNEY THOMPSON / JACK THURSTON / BILL WENZEL / STAN BORACK / JACK BRESLOW / DAN
McCANCE / SAUL MANDEL / LOU MARCHETTI / RITA FLODEN LEYDON / JERRY PODWIL / WHITNEY DARR
R POPP / DICK POWERS / GENE SZAFRAN / HERB TAUSS / GEORGE SOTTUNG / HAL SEIGEL / WALTER ST
N SCHWALB / DICK KENNERSON / ELAINE DUILLO / DEAN ELLIS / TOM MILLER / CHARLIE MOLL / MIKE STRO
McDERMOTT / BOB McGINNIS / ED McLAUGHLIN / ALAN MAGEE / MARA McAFEE / PAUL BACON / JO
LIEBLEIN / OSCAR LIEBMAN / JOE LOMBARDERO / JOHN BERKEY / CHARLIE MOLL / BOB CUEVAS / ANN D
R PREZIO / DON PUNCHATZ / DORIS RODEWIG / HOWARD ROGERS / DON MOSS / BIL KEANE / HANK
HOOKS / CHET JEZIERSKI / BILL JOHNSON / STUART KAUFMAN / NORMAN ADAMS / HECTOR GARRIDO /
MAGUIRE / FRANK FRAZETTA / STAN GALLI / CHARLIE GEHM / ALLAN MARDON / RONNIE LESSER / JACK D
KNIGHT / DICK KOHFIELD / ROLF ERIKSON / CARL HANTMAN / JOHNNY HART / HARRY KANE / MORT KU
LODEN LEYDON / PETER CARAS / JOHN CHILLY / TED COCONIS / GIL COHEN / LEW McCANCE / GENE

FAWCETT

Joel Snyder

© craven & evans CREATIVE GRAPHICS

880 Third Avenue, New York, N.Y. 10022, Telephone 212-421-6808

A complete service to publishers in design, illustration and production

Illustrators—Robert Altemus Armando Baez
Bini Bichisecchi Brian Bourke Richard Brown
Beth Charney Marilyn Cohen Olivia H. H. Cole
Bob Cram Margaret Cranstoun Jim Crowell
Angela Fernan Denver Gillen Susan Gilmour
Bob Giuliani Judy Glasser Risa Glickman
David Grove Meryl Henderson Tom Hill
Nicole Hollander Charles Jakubowski
Judy Kanis Laurie Kaufman Marion Krupp
Valdis Kupris Roberta Langman
Peter Lehndorff Yee Lin Sven Lindman
Ken Longtemps Hal Lose Anita Lovitt
Eleanor Mill Victor Mojica Carl Molno

Jay Moon Larry Morelli Dale Moyer
Sal Murdocca Mike Nakai Kelly Oechsli
Robert Owens Ted Rand Gilbert Riswold
Christopher Santoro Roz Schanzer Joel Schick
Den Schofield Leonard Shalansky Diane Shapiro
Charles Shaw Robert Shore Ed Sibbitt
Dorothea Sierra Dick Smith Joel Snyder
Jim Stewart John Swatsley Susanne Valla
Charles Walker Ron Walotsky Karen Watson
Jeff Zinggeler **Photographers**—George Ancona
Curtis Blake Joel Gordon Michal Heron
Molly Heron Stephen Maka Joan Menschenfreund
George Roos Dick Smith Joel Weltman

artists

NORMAN ADAMS / KEVIN BROOKS / DAVID BYRD / BOB HANDVILLE
NORMAN LALIBERTE / DENNIS LUCZAK / JIM MANOS
ALLAN MARDON / JACK MARTIN / FRED OTNES / GENE SZAFRAN
REPRESENTED BY BILL ERLACHER / PHILIP CANADY
ARTISTS ASSOCIATES / 211 E. 51 ST. / NEW YORK, N.Y. 10022 / 212 755-1365/6

OUR TEN COMMANDMENTS OF REPPING

1. Represent only talent you believe in.
2. Appreciate the problems of your artists and try whenever possible to eliminate the problems of your talent.
3. Appreciate the problems of the art director: his client-agency relationship, tight deadlines, budget limitations. Try to eliminate or expedite these problems for the AD.
4. Be more than an agent. Be interested in the artist's whole career.
5. Give **full** representation. That means not taking on too many people, or making too few personal calls. You cannot sell fifty artists over the telephone.
6. Give service promptly and gladly. Every client, no matter what price the job, deserves the best.
7. BE HONEST . . . with your talent . . . with the art director . . . with yourself.
8. Be flexible. Business conditions change. The economy rises and falls. Accounts switch. Control those things you can control, but recognize what you cannot control and adjust your psyche accordingly.
9. **Always** meet deadlines and **always** keep a bargain. You are only as good as your word and only as good as your last job.
10. **Enjoy your work.** Repping is one of the most exciting and stimulating fields I know of. It has its problems, but these problems are vastly outweighed by the challenges and pleasures. When repping stops being fun—leave.

Barbara Gordon
Associates Ltd.
165 East 32 Street
New York, N.Y. 10016
212-686-3514

Barbara and Elliott Gordon
Representing Bart Forbes/James Barkley/Margaret Cusack/
Sandy Huffaker/Victor Valla/Sandy Hoffman/Bob Brown/
Keita Colton/Ron Barry

SUBMIT YOUR SAMPLES TO:
EDITORIAL ART DEPARTMENT, 10TH FLOOR
PLAYBOY MAGAZINE
919 NORTH MICHIGAN AVENUE
CHICAGO, ILLINOIS 60611

(MAIL SLIDES OR PHOTOGRAPHY—NO ORIGINAL ART, PLEASE)

We hope we're in your book

MORT DRUCKER

CHARLES SANTORE

KEN PANCIERA

JACK DAVIS

DICK ANDERSON

STU LEUTHNER

THE EINSELS

JACQUI MORGAN

BRUCE STARK

NORMAN DOHERTY

TONY GABRIELE

BOB SCHULENBERG

JOSEPH VENO

CAL SACKS

RAYMOND KURSAR

DAVID GAADT

Behind the truly outstanding art you'l

ind Frank and Jeff Lavaty.

You'll find contemporary and nostalgic styles treating all subjects.
Individual portfolios are available from the following artists
represented exclusively by Frank and Jeff Lavaty.

John Berkey, Bernard D'Andrea, Rolland des Combes, Chris Duke,
James Flora, Lorraine Fox, Gervasio Gallardo, Blake Hampton,
Stan Hunter, Chet Jezierski, Larry Kresek, Mort Kunstler,
Lemuel Line, Robert Lo Grippo, Robert Schulz, Paul Williams.

Representative booklet of 100 color examples available for your file.
Phone (212) 355-0910. Or write Frank and Jeff Lavaty,
45 East 51st St., N.Y., N.Y. 10022.

ART & ILLUSTRATION

ART

FRANK & JEFF LAVATY — ARTIST REPRESENTATIVES
45 EAST 51st STREET, N.Y., N.Y. 22 **PHONE 212-355-0910**

art staff inc.

Advertising Art Specialists

369 Lexington Avenue
New York, New York 10017

Tel. (212) 867·2660

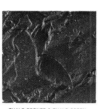
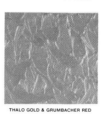

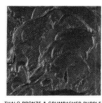
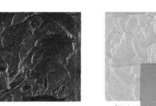

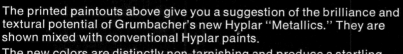

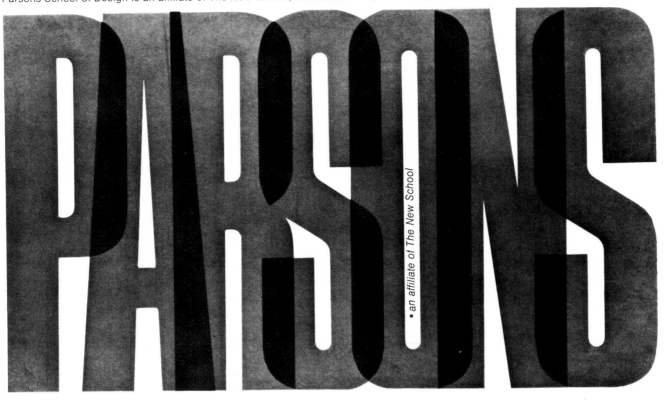

Representing
Illustrators
To Publishers
Of Children's
Materials

Send For
Your
Brochure
Of Artists
Samples

By Diane Dawson One Of My Many Fine Illustrators

ANNOUNCING

CAROL
BANCROFT
AND
FRIENDS

1A Putnam Green Greenwich Connecticut 06830 203 531·1741

Larry Noble, one of the many fine artists represented exclusively by...

ALAN E. COBER

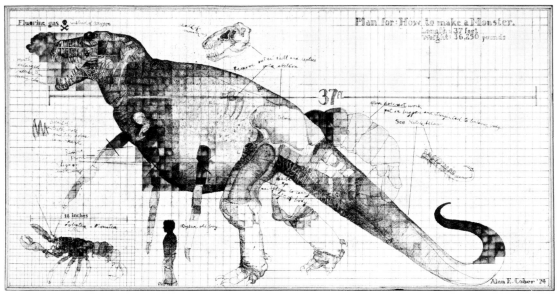

1975 Gold Medal Editorial Illustration   Publication: Boys' Life Magazine

1975 Award of Excellence Advertising Illustration   Client: National Park Service

Gerald & Cullen Rapp are proud
to represent Alan E. Cober
recipient of eight major awards from
The Society of Illustrators
in the past six years.

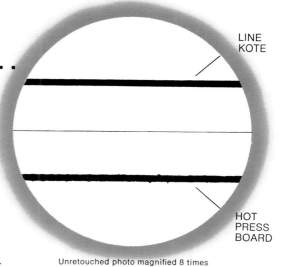

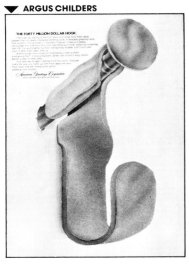

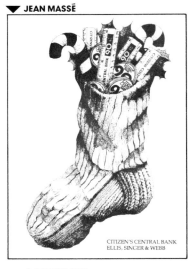
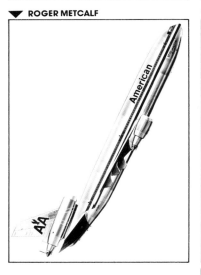

OUR DOOR IS ALWAYS OPEN

Artwork is an essential part of our business, and during the course of years we have worked with some of the most distinguished artists, illustrators and designers in the world. At the right is a partial list.

Western Publishing Company, Inc., through its various divisions, publishes and prints a wide variety of books for adults and children, as well as periodicals, educational material, games, playing cards, toys and other packaged items.

Our door is always open to creative people. Write, call, or drop in at any of our offices in New York, Los Angeles, or Racine, Wisconsin.

Western Publishing Company, Inc.

Publishing imprints: GOLDEN PRESS • WHITMAN

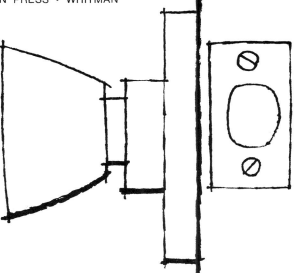

John Alcorn
Joan Anglund
Aurelius Battaglia
Shielah Beckett
Ludwig Bemmelmans
Harry Bennett
Eugene Berman
Lawrence Bjorklund
Mary Blair
Bob Blechman
Eric Blegvad
Niels Bodecker
Seymour Chwast
Herbert Danska
Cornelius DeWitt
Ann Ophelia Dowden
Gertrude Elliot
Dean Ellis
Robert Fawcett
Helen Federico
Betty Fraser
Antonio Frasconi
Gyo Fujikawa
Tibor Gergerly
George Giusti
Denver Gillen
Lou Glanzman
Milton Glaser
Simon Greco
Charles Harper
Don Helm
Homer Hill
Clark Hulings
Scott Johnston
Carroll Jones
Leonard Kalish
Joe Kaufman
Howard Koslow
Robert Kuhn
Robert J. Lee
James Lewicki
Walter Linsenmaier
Harry McNaught
Tran Mawicke
Rebecca Merrilees
John Paar Miller
Yoko Mitsuhashi
Susan Perl
Barry Phillips
Richard Powers
Alice and Martin Proven
Albert John Pucci
Harlow Rockwell
Feodor Rojankovsky
Richard Scarry
Dan Schwartz
Ben Shahn
Robert Shore
Arthur Singer
Lawrence Beale Smith
Edward Sorrell
Peter Spier
David Stone
William Teason
Gustav Tenggrenn
Murray Tinkelman
Alton Tobey
Leonard Weisgard
Eloise Wilkin
Garth Williams
Rudy Zallinger

JESSIE NEELEY

JESSIE NEELEY ARTIST REPRESENTATIVE 575-1234

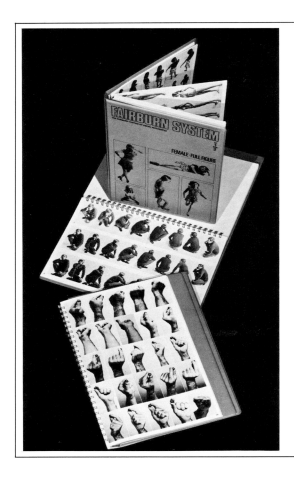

We're scouting Heavy Hitters

Illustrators with promising batting averages. With big-league potential. With the drive & desire to rate someday with Bernard Fuchs, Bob Peak or Mark English.

Pitt Studios' range of consumer and institutional accounts offers plenty of chances to swing away. We seldom bunt.

Pitt (55 years in Cleveland and Pittsburgh) is the largest studio in our part of the world. We're looking for illustrators who can render line & wash, B&W & color. Make crisp layout indications and finished art. Draw figures well.

Don't wait for our scouts to find you. Send samples (on slides, please) to Carl W. Behl, President, Pitt Studios, 1430 Northern Ohio Bank Building, Cleveland, Ohio 44113. Or phone collect: 216/241-6720.

Run-producers come in any age. But we need illustrators with at least 3 years' experience.

*choose the right board... and your job's off to a good start.

Yes, there is a right surface...
a BAINBRIDGE BOARD...
for every medium and technique

#172 is smooth	#80 is medium

and Bainbridge Genuine Studio Drawing Bristol (smooth and medium) for fine and commercial art work.

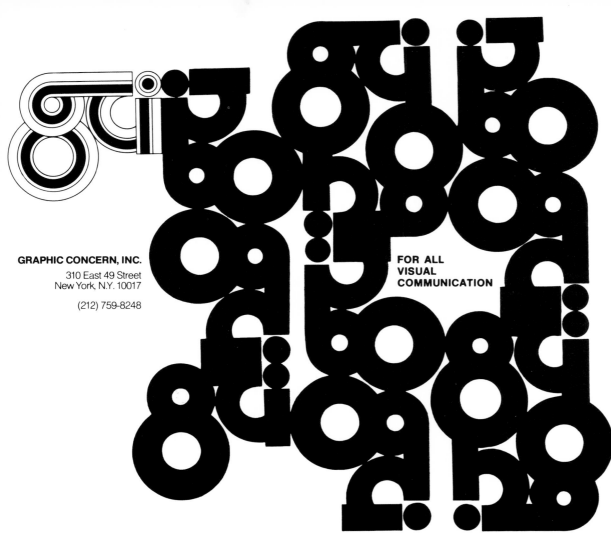

GRAPHIC CONCERN, INC.
310 East 49 Street
New York, N.Y. 10017

(212) 759-8248

**FOR ALL
VISUAL
COMMUNICATION**

A COMPLETE SERVICE
TO PUBLISHERS IN
GRAPHIC DESIGN, ART
AND PRODUCTION
OF EL-HI, JUVENILE
AND EDUCATIONAL
MATERIALS

*Book Design
Jacket and Cover Design
Illustrations and Photography
Project Design
Package Design
Corporate Design
Promotion and Mailing Pieces
Booklets and Brochures
Trademarks*

Index

While every effort has been made to insure the accuracy of the credits in this volume, it is inevitable that an occasional error may have crept in. On behalf of the Society of Illustrators, the publishers would appreciate information about any omissions or corrections. As this book is printed in process colors, we regret that the original colors of some of the illustrations reproduced here have been altered.

Production Credits

The text in this book is: Souvenir Demi with Light

Composition by: M. J. Baumwell, Typography

Offset plates and printing by: Connecticut Printers, Inc.

Advertisements section by: Bodley Printers, Inc.

The paper is: Mead's Black and White Offset Enamel Dull

Paper supplier: Andrews/Nelson/Whitehead Publishing Papers

Binding cloth by: G.S.B. Fabrics Corp.

Bound by: A. Horowitz and Son

Jacket printed by: Princeton Polychrome Press

Production Supervision: Lee Tobin, Hastings House

Assistant to the publisher: James Moore, Hastings House

INDEX

ILLUSTRATORS

ART DIRECTORS

AGENCIES

TITLES

FILM PRODUCER

FILM PRODUCTION, see under **AGENCIES**